PROBLEM SOLVING
WITH CALCULATORS

PROBLEM SOLVING WITH CALCULATORS

Karen Billings
and
David Moursund

dilithium Press
Portland, Oregon

ISBN: 0-918398-30-4
Library of Congress catalog card number: 79-56398

Printed in the United States of America.

dilithium Press
P.O. Box 92
Forest Grove, Oregon 97116

PREFACE FOR TEACHERS

The National Council of Teachers of Mathematics, The National Council of Supervisors of Mathematics, and many mathematics education leaders have gone on record supporting the use of calculators in schools. Both *The Arithmetic Teacher* and *The Mathematics Teacher* regularly carry articles on uses of calculators. Many new mathematics textbook series contain some discussion of calculators and problems designed to be done with a calculator.

It is not sufficient for students today to simply possess good computational skills. They must learn to apply these skills in problem solving situations. Problem solving is the first and foremost goal in mathematics education.

This book is designed to help secondary school students learn about calculators and to improve their problem solving skills. No knowledge of math beyond a sixth grade level is assumed. However, the book touches upon a number of topics typically taught at a secondary school pre-algebra level. The new material in these topics is explained at an intuitive level and by examples. There is extensive instruction on the ideas and methods of problem solving.

Students using this book must have a calculator in hand, as well as pencil and paper. The emphasis is upon learning by doing. About two-thirds of the content is exercises and activities.

The chapters are divided into short sections. A typical student can complete a section in one or two days. Most sections consist of about one page of written explanation followed by several pages of exercises and activities. It is not necessary to complete every exercise before proceeding to the next section. Rather, the exercises are designed to meet the needs of a wide range of students. Students with a high level of mathematical ability and with adequate time will be able to complete all of the exercises. Those with a lower level of ability and/or less time will complete only the first few exercises. But this is adequate for proceeding to the next section.

It is important to realize that there are many different types of calculators, with significant differences in their features. You, and this book, can help students to learn some of the similarities and differences among various calculators. Students should experience the use of several different brands and models.

If your school or your students are going to purchase calculators, then we have the following recommendations.

1. Purchase an LCD (liquid crystal display) rather than an LED (light emitting diode) calculator. This virtually eliminates the problem of batteries wearing out.

2. Purchase a calculator with a simple memory system. The calculator memory chapter of this book emphasizes the four key memory system. This is a system that has M+, M−, CM, and RM keys.

3. Purchase a calculator that uses algebraic logic. Such a calculator has an = key and does not have an ENT key. (An ENT key is essential to a "Reverse Polish Notation" calculator, often used in more advanced science and engineering work.)

4. Purchase a calculator that has only a limited number of function keys other than +, −, ×, and ÷. This book makes mention of a square root key, but that is not an essential feature. No other special function keys are discussed.

5. Purchase a calculator that does not use scientific notation and which is not programmable.

To summarize, an inexpensive, 8-digit, non-programmable, algebraic logic, LCD calculator with a simple memory system is most appropriate to use with this book. You can expect to pay about $12 to $18 for such a machine.

This book is designed to be used in three different modes. It can be used in a self-contained course, perhaps 9 to 12 weeks in length. Or, it can be used to supplement a longer course. If materials from this book are used once or twice per week, they will supplement a year-long course. Finally, the book is suitable for self-instruction. Students can work through it at their own pace, completing as many sections as their time and interest permit.

PREFACE FOR STUDENTS

Calculators are now commonplace. They are available in most homes, schools, and places of business. Almost all math education leaders agree that students should learn how to use calculators and should be allowed to use them in school.

This book has two main purposes. One is to help you learn about calculators. The second purpose is to help improve your math problem solving skills. A calculator can improve your speed and accuracy at doing complex calculations, but calculation is only a small part of mathematics. What to calculate, when to calculate, and the meaning of the results are more important.

Problem solving involves understanding of problems, figuring out how to solve them, and then carrying out solution processes; it requires careful thinking. Through study and practice you can improve your problem solving skills.

This book contains many exercises and activities. It should be studied with a calculator as well as pencil and paper at hand. You will quickly learn that there are many kinds of calculators and that they differ significantly. It is important that you learn how to use different calculators. If you are planning to buy a calculator, first read PREFACE FOR TEACHERS and the first chapter of this book for some helpful information.

CONTENTS

GETTING STARTED

LOOK AT YOUR CALCULATOR

Have you ever used a calculator? Probably you have, since they are now so common. Most schools, homes, and places of business have calculators. They are inexpensive, and they are easy to use.

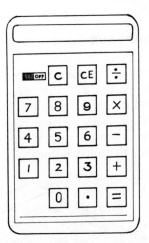

This book is designed to be studied with a calculator in hand. Compare your calculator with the one pictured. In what ways do they appear to be the same? In what ways are they different? As you study this book, you will learn that all calculators are not alike. Indeed, there are major and important differences.

Turn on your calculator and fill the display with numbers. How many digits can it display? An 8-digit display is most common. A calculator with an 8-digit display is called an 8 digit calculator. Push the C (clear) key. (Some calculators have a key labeled C/CE . If yours is of this type, push that key twice.) This clears the display, setting it to zero. To correct a keying error, push the CE (clear entry) key. Practice using the clear and clear entry keys.

Check to see if your calculator has an = key. If it does, then most likely your machine is an algebraic logic calculator and is the type discussed in this book. If it does not, then your calculator uses Reverse Polish Notation (RPN) logic. Many of the more expensive calculators used by scientists and engineers use RPN. However, we will only be discussing algebraic logic calculators in this book.

Experiment with your calculator. For example, push the keys

$$2 \quad 7 \quad + \quad 5 \quad 6 \quad =$$

This display should show 83. Try out the various keys on your calculator. Are there any that you can't figure out? Make a note to yourself about them and see if you can learn how they work with further reading.

CALCULATOR DISPLAYS

A calculator can display the numbers you key in and the answer it produces. Some calculators print these numbers on paper. They are called *hard copy* output calculators, and they are commonly used in business. Hard copy output calculators are generally more expensive than *video display* calculators, which use small lights to display output.

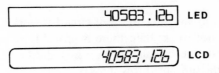

There are two common types of video displays. The light emitting diode (LED) display glows red or green in the dark, and drains batteries very rapidly. A set of batteries may last only 10-15 hours in an LED calculator. The liquid crystal display (LCD) depends upon reflected light. A set of batteries may last 1000-2000 hours or more in an LCD calculator.

POWER SOURCE

Calculators use electricity. This electricity can come from a wall socket or from batteries. Some calculators are made to use both sources.

The most common, and cheapest, calculators use disposable batteries. One throws the batteries away after they are used up. A battery powered LED calculator usually uses small penlight batteries such as are used in small flashlights, or a 9 volt battery such as is common in transistor radios. An LCD calculator can make use of much smaller, thin batteries, like those used in electronic digital watches. Thus, an LCD calculator is apt to be thinner and smaller than an LED calculator. Indeed, some LCD calculators are little thicker than a credit card.

Certain types of calculator batteries can be recharged. When the batteries start to run down, one merely plugs the charger into a wall socket for a few hours or overnight. Rechargeable batteries tend to wear out after a year or two of service, and so are not the bargain they first seem.

IS IT WORKING RIGHT?

Please turn on your calculator. Is it working right? The first thing to check is the display. If your machine has a video display then it should light up when the calculator is turned on. Probably it will display the number 0. What the display looks like when the calculator is first turned on will vary with the machine being used.

If the display on your calculator is not working right, the first thing to check is the power source. If it uses batteries, put in a fresh set. If the calculator needs 110 volts AC, make sure it is plugged in and that the wall circuit is working. If the display still does not work, then there is probably something seriously wrong with the calculator. You may decide to ship it back to the manufacturer or throw it away.

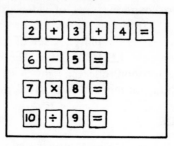

If the display is working right, run a few tests using each of the keys to check out the circuitry. Do some simple calculations, like those in the box. Notice that each can be done mentally so the calculator answer can be checked.

Before each calculation push the **C** (clear) key. (If you calculator has a **C/CE** key, then push it twice.) This erases, or clears the previous calculation from the calculator's circuitry, and puts a 0. in the display.

```
       1 . 1 1 1 etc.
    9 ) 1 0 . 0 0 0
        9
        ─────
        1 0
          9
        ─────
        1 0
```

The division problem $10 \div 9$ should produce a string of digits after the decimal point. On an 8-digit calculator, the display will read 1.1111111, which is the first eight digits of the answer. Try some other division, such as $2 \div 3$, to see how the calculator displays the answer.

TESTING 1, 2, 3 . . .

Here are two math tests on whole numbers. They are the same level of difficulty. See how well you can do when using paper and pencil, then using a calculator.

Do Test A using paper and pencil and see how long it takes you to finish.

A. 1. 932   2. 8664   3. 30$\overline{)7020}$ 4. 54   5. 115
       $\times$ 7 -3273 $\times 20$ 47
                                                                          53
                                                                          19
                                                                          82
    6. 6$\overline{)9865}$ 7. 89 + 7 + 25 =   6
                                                                       + 8

    8. 85432 − 2789   9. 30 × 570   10. 604 ÷ 4

Do Test B using a calculator to get the answers. Time yourself.

B. 1. 815   2. 3785   3. 40$\overline{)6080}$ 4.   31   5. 200
       $\times$ 6 -1394 $\times 30$ 73
                                                                          62
                                                                          18
                                                                          91
    6. 5$\overline{)6729}$ 7. 77 + 8 + 306   7
                                                                       + 5

    8. 68873 − 4678   9. 40 × 460   10. 804 ÷ 3

Now check your answers and compare your two scores. Even if you have never used a calculator before you are apt to discover that your speed and accuracy using it exceeded your pencil and paper skills.

CALCULATOR LETTERS

A calculator is a machine designed to work with numbers. However, when the video display is turned upside down most of the digits look like letters.

Calculator Digit	0	1	2	3	4	5	6	7	8	9
Upside-down Digit	0	1	Z	E	h	5	9	L	8	-

These letters can be made into words like "Shell oil," and used to play word games on a calculator.

6   Problem Solving with Calculators

Try these problems.

What did the cannibal cook say when asked if supper was ready? To find out: Find the product of 6 and 4759. Add .17. Double the result.	What did the Red Baron put into Snoopy's house? To find out: Multiply one hundred and one by the square of three. Add fifty. Multiply the result by each of the whole numbers between six and nine exclusive.
What did Amelia Earhart's father say the first time he saw her flying an airplane by herself? To find out: Find .023 × 3. Add 10141 to the result. Multiply by 5.	What does Billie Jean King do to win her tennis matches? To find out: Find the square of 11. Subtract 15.521. Multiply by 5. Multiply by the square root of 121.

Do you know how to make up problems to get answers like "HOLES" on the calculator? You first need to know the numbers that produce these letters. Use the chart or trial and error to help you.

0	I	2	3	4	5	6	7	8	9
0	I	Z	E	h	S	9	L	B	-

S	3	7	0	4
5	3	7	0	4

Now we need to work backwards and make up a mathematical problem that has 53704 as an answer.

Here are some one step problems with that answer. Use your calculator or mental arithmetic to finish each problem.

A. 33000 + _____ = 53704   C. 4 × _____ = 53704

B. 1000000 − _____ = 53704   D. _____ ÷ 3 = 53704

Calculate 3000 + 67 + 5 + 202 + 50430. This is one way to make the problem longer. However, if you study the previous page you will notice that different operations (and sometimes all four) were used in the short stories. To make up these problems, use a technique called working backwards.

Let's extend problem A from above:

$$33000 + 20704.$$

(Select two numbers to get 33000.)

Multiply 4125 by ____. Add 20704.

(Select two numbers to get 4125.)

Subtract 875 from ____. Multiply it by ____. Add 20704.

(Select two numbers to get 5000.)

Divide ____ by ____. Subtract 875. Multiply it by ____. Add 20704.

Try this process with problems B or C or D for more practice.

NOW IT'S YOUR TURN

1. Make a list of all two letter calculator words (go, be, oh, . . .). When in doubt, check with a dictionary.
2. Make up two different sequences of calculations that produce the word gobble. Then make up a question to go with that answer.
3. Work with one or two other people. Make as long a list as possible of calculator words and/or phrases. Combine your list with those of other students to make a large collection.
4. Make up two different sequences of calculations that produce the phrase "he.lies". Think of a question or statement to go with it.
5. The word "geologizes" is 10 characters long and can be displayed by a 10-digit calculator. Find additional words or phrases that use 10 or more calculator characters.
6. Several different companies now make calculators that contain both numeric and alphabetic keys. A typical calculator of this type can store up to 30 words or short phrases. These remain in the machine's memory even after it is turned off.

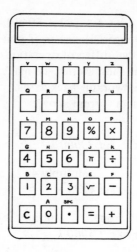

What are the advantages and disadvantages of this "scratch pad" calculator versus paper and pencil for storing short written messages?

SOME SYMMETRIES

Look at the numbers from 0 to 9 on your calculator right side up and upside down. The 0 looks the same when you read it from both directions. Do any other numbers have this property?

Many geometric figures have a center point, and remain unchanged if rotated 180° about the center point. That is, they have point symmetry. Rotating a figure 180° is the same as turning it upside down. The calculator number 6889 has point symmetry. The point of symmetry is located between the two 8's.

1. What do these calculator numbers become when rotated 180°?

   81 ____   818 ____   181 ____   619 ____

   For those having point symmetry, indicate the point of symmetry.

2. What is the smallest two-digit number you can display with point symmetry?

3. Find some eight-digit numbers with point symmetry. What are the smallest and largest of these?

4. List the years from 1000 A.D. to the present with point symmetry.

Line symmetry is defined by a motion called reflection. Some of the single digits have one or two lines of symmetry. (Most calculator digits are slightly slanted to make them easier to read. Pretend the slant does not exist.)

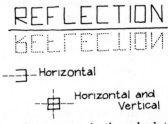

Notice the lines of symmetry in the calculator numbers 3 and 8. What is another digit with line symmetry.

A number of several digits can have line symmetry. Draw in the vertical lines of symmetry in these numbers.

1. What is the smallest two-digit number you can display with line symmetry?
2. Find the smallest and largest eight digit numbers on your calculator with line symmetry.
3. What are the years since 1000 A.D. with line symmetry?
4. Do all calculator numbers with a vertical line of symmetry also have a horizontal line of symmetry?
5. Does every calculator number with a horizontal line of symmetry have a vertical line of symmetry also?

TRANSLATION → TRANSLATION

Slide symmetry is produced by a motion called translation. For example, the number 1111 is formed by repeated translation or "slide" of the digit "1."

List all of the counting numbers that you can make on your calculator by translating the digit "1."

If you made the same kind of list for the other single digits (2 through 9), how many total numbers could be produced? Try these on your calculator.

1. Find the decimal equivalent for

$$\frac{1}{9} \qquad \frac{2}{9} \qquad \frac{3}{9}$$

.33333333 can also be written as $.\overline{3}$ (the repeating number is placed under the horizontal bar).
Predict the decimal display for

$$\frac{5}{9} \qquad \frac{8}{9}$$

Check it on your calculator.

2. Find the decimal equivalents for these fractions.

$$\frac{11}{99} \quad \frac{25}{99} \quad \frac{67}{99} \quad \frac{8}{99} \quad \frac{121}{999} \quad \frac{566}{999} \quad \frac{834}{999} \quad \frac{25}{999}$$

Predict, then check, decimals for

$$\frac{37}{99} \quad \frac{522}{999} \quad \frac{7}{99} \quad \frac{62}{999} \quad \frac{5663}{9999} \quad \frac{847}{9999}$$

3. Several digits may be used in a translation, such as 121121. This number is formed from 121 by a slide transformation. List all of the years since 1000 A. D. with slide symmetry.

4. What is the most recent year that could be produced by a rotation; reflection; translation?

ORDER OF OPERATIONS

How would you work this problem:

$$5 + 2 \times 8$$

One person may say that it's 7×8 or 56, while another says it's $5 + 16$ or 21. Which one is right? Unless we agree on the meaning of the symbols, we may never agree on the answer! To take care of this situation, mathematicians have agreed that the meaning of $5 + 2 \times 8$ is $5 + (2 \times 8)$.

They have decided on some general rules concerning the order of operations. They are as follows:

1. Work from left to right, doing each multiplication and division problem as you come to it.

2. Go back and work from left to right again doing each addition and subtraction problem as you come to it.

$$5 + 2 \times 8$$
$$= 5 + (2 \times 8)$$
$$= 5 + 16$$
$$= 21$$

Example: Evaluate this expression:

$$46 - 3 \times 2 + 8 \div 4 \times 5$$

Use Rule 1 $46 - 3 \times 2 + 8 \div 4 \times 5$ *Rule 2* $46 - 6 + 10$
$\downarrow$ $\downarrow$

$46 -$ **6** $+ 8 \div 4 \times 5$ **40** $+ 10$
$\downarrow$ $\downarrow$

$46 -$ 6 $+$ **2** $\times 5$ **50**
$\downarrow$

$46 -$ 6 $+$ **10**   *Go To*

Often people use parentheses to make the order of operations clear. The above expressions could be written as

$$46 - (3 \times 2) + ((8 \div 4) \times 5)$$

Mathematicians have also agreed that the work inside parentheses should be done first. If there are parentheses within parentheses (as in our example) work from the inside out. You would calculate $((8 \div 4) \times 5)$
$\downarrow$
(2×5)
$\downarrow$
10

1. Insert parentheses into the following expressions, following the established rules. Then evaluate each expression (do the operations) with the help of your calculator, paper and pencil and/or mental arithmetic.

   a. $5 + 3 \times 8$ e. $64 - 64 \times 8$
   b. $93.7 - 16.2 \times 5$ f. $792 - 92 + 108 - 8$
   c. $37 \times 6.4 - 120.5$ g. $108 \div 6 \times 94 - 16$
   d. $75 \div 6 - 9 \div 2$ h. $1728 \div 12 \div 12 \div 12$

2. After doing a number of calculations like above, one is able to mentally insert parentheses. Carry out the following calculations without actually writing in the parentheses. (Just "think" them in.)

   a. $89.4 + 27 \times 16.1$ _____
   b. $184 \div 8 + 17.2$ _____
   c. $1728 \div 12 \div 12 + 5$ _____
   d. $8.42 \times 5 + 17.9$ _____
   e. $-14.2 + 76.1 \times 7$ _____

The correct sum of the above answers is 1159.8

3. Insert parentheses, then find the missing numbers in each of the following equations.

     a. ____ × 17 = 323
     b. 3 × ____ + 8 = 23
     c. 6 × ____ − 89 = 79
     d. 84 + 7 × ____ = 280
     e. 493 ÷ ____ + 8 = 37
     f. ____ + 27 × 43 = 1200
     g. 69 × 8 − ____ = 2

EXPONENTS EXPLAINED

3^5 is a concise way of writing $3 \times 3 \times 3 \times 3 \times 3$. It is read "three to the fifth power." The 3 is called the base number and it is used as a factor five times.

One way to find 3^5 on a calculator is to key in

$$\boxed{3}\ \boxed{\times}\ \boxed{3}\ \boxed{\times}\ \boxed{3}\ \boxed{\times}\ \boxed{3}\ \boxed{\times}\ \boxed{3}\ \boxed{=}$$

but most calculators have an automatic constant for multiplication which makes the calculation easier. Try keying in the following on your calculator.

$$\boxed{3}\ \boxed{\times}\ \boxed{=}\ \boxed{=}\ \boxed{=}\ \boxed{=}$$

Do you get 243, the same answer as above? If so, your calculator has an automatic constant for multiplication. Find these powers using your calculator or mentally.

2^{10}	3^{15}	9^8	14^5	1.5^6
10^2	10^3	10^6	10^{10}	10^{14}

How can you find powers of 10 without a calculator or paper and pencil?

1. Look at the powers of 5 5^1 5^4
    The last digit is always 5^2 5^5
    what number? 5^3 5^6

2. Look at the successive powers of the other one-digit numbers. The last digit repeats with which of those numbers?

3. What is the last digit in 7^{100}? To solve this problem, look for a pattern in the successive powers of seven.

$7^1 = 7$ $7^5 = $ 7^9 will end in ___

$7^2 = 49$ $7^6 = $ 7^{10} will end in ___

$7^3 = $ $7^7 = $ Where will 7^{100} fit into the pattern?

$7^4 = $ $7^8 = $

4. What is the next-to-last digit in 7^{100}?

OPERATIONS WITH POWERS

A complicated mathematical expression may involve parentheses and exponents as well as addition, subtraction, multiplication, and division. If a calculation involves parentheses, then work within the parentheses first. Next do the powers.

$2^4 + 3^2$	$(2^4 + 3)^2$	$(2^4 + 3) \times 2$
↓	↓	↓
$16 + 9$	$(16 + 3)^2$	$(16 + 3) \times 2$
↓	↓	↓
25	$(19^2) = 361$	$(19) \times 2 = 38$

Here is the general order of operations (going from left to right at each step):

a. parentheses
b. powers
c. multiply and divide
d. add and subtract

I remember the order with "Pretty Please my dear Aunt Sally".

A good way to remember the order of operations is with the sentence "Pretty Please My Dear Aunt Sally." The first letter of each word used in the sentence is the same as the first letter of the operations. Pretty = parenthesis; Please = powers, My =

multiply, etc. This type of sentence is called a mnemonic (pronounce knee-mon-ic). Mnemonics help you to remember unfamiliar things by associating them with an easy to remember word or phrase.

1. Practice the general order of operations on the following calculations:

   a. $(9 + 7)^3$ e. $5^2 - 4^2$

   b. $9^3 + 7$ f. $13^2 - 12^2$

   c. $9 + 7^3$ g. $31^2 - 30^2$

   d. $9^3 + 7^3$ h. Look for a pattern in the answers to
                          e–g. Use it to find $73^2 - 72^2$. Check
                          your answer.

2. Complete this chart:

$$1^3 = 1$$
$$1^3 + 2^3 = 9$$
$$1^3 + 2^3 + 3^3 =$$
$$1^3 + 2^3 + 3^3 + 4^3 =$$
$$1^3 + 2^3 + 3^3 + 4^3 + 5^3 =$$

Predict

$$1^3 + 2^3 + 3^3 + \ldots + 10^3 =$$

Hint: The numbers on the right are perfect squares.

CHAINING

A calculation involving a sequence of operations, such as $8 + 9 - 5 =$, is called a chain calculation. Key this calculation into your machine and observe the output display. Video display calculators display the intermediate answers in an addition/subtraction chain. That is, the sequence $8 + 9 -$ is treated exactly as if it were $8 + 9 = -$. The intermediate answer 17 is displayed.

Examine how your calculator handles the chain calculation $8 + 2 \times 9 =$. Many calculators will treat the sequence $8 + 2 \times$ exactly as if it were $8 + 2 = \times$. Thus they produce an intermediate answer of 10 and a final answer of 90. This final answer is mathematically incorrect according to the rules we studied earlier.

Now you can see why it is necessary to understand the rules for order of operations and to develop skill at inserting parentheses. Failure to do so will result in incorrect calculator answers with many calculators. When you see a calculation such as 8 + 2 × 9 =, you should think to yourself that the actual calculation to be done is 8 + (2 × 9). On most calculators this must be done in the order (2 × 9) + 8 in order to get the correct answer.

But not all calculators are built this way. On some calculators the sequence 8 + 2 × 9 = will produce the mathematically correct answer of 26. Such calculators are "smart" enough to realize that a chain with a mixture of × and ÷ with + and − must be treated differently. Such a calculator has circuitry that automatically treats this example as 8 + (2 × 9) =. That is, the circuitry inserts the necessary parentheses. Test your calculator to see if it has this capability. Be aware that most calculators do not have that capability.

1. Key 5 + 4 × 8 = into your calculator. Is the result mathematically correct?

2. Repeat the above experiment using the calculation 23 − 18 ÷ 6 = .

3. A student wants to find the sum

$$\frac{1}{2} + \frac{1}{2}$$

on a calculator. The student keys in 1 ÷ 2 + 1 ÷ 2 = and gets .75 as an answer. Explain why this incorrect answer occurs. Hint: Insert parentheses into the sequence 1 ÷ 2 + 1 ÷ 2 = to show the order of operations that the calculator used.

4. The same calculator is used to try to find the sum of

$$\frac{1}{3} + \frac{1}{3} + \frac{1}{3}$$

The student keys in 1 ÷ 3 + 1 ÷ 3 + 1 ÷ 3 =. What does the student get? Insert parentheses to show the order of operations that the calculator used.

5. Mentally calculate what your calculator will produce from the sequence 1 ÷ 2 + 1 ÷ 2 + 1 ÷ 2 = . Check using your calculator.

PROBLEM SOLVING

WHAT ARE PROBLEMS?

Most math teachers agree that the main goal in math education is to learn to solve problems. But what does it mean to solve problems? What is a problem? Recently a group of students in a math class were asked to give examples of problems. They were encouraged to describe general problems and were not restricted just to math. They gave examples such as the following:

$$22 + 87 + 13 + 128 \qquad\qquad 943.8\overline{)892164.56}$$

$$\frac{183.7^3 - 64.9^4}{17.2^5}$$

$$\begin{array}{r} \$87.35 \\ 6.29 \\ 13.62 \\ 4.65 \\ +12.80 \\ \hline \end{array}$$

$$\sqrt{178.3}$$

Each of these is an example of a problem. But these are very limited examples. Each one is a math problem. Moreover, each one is an arithmetic calculation problem.

No one thought of examples from geometry. Here are two examples.

1. Find the area and perimeter
   of this rectangle.

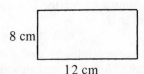

2. Remove 4 of these toothpicks so that four equal triangles remain. No loose
toothpicks may be left.

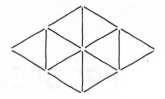

REAL PROBLEMS

No one thought of applications outside the field of mathematics. Here are some examples of problem situations that
involve numbers or geometry.

1. In the United States approximately 6% of the people who
would like to have a job are out of work. Government officials
would like this figure to be reduced to below 4%. This means
that they would like to find employment for about 2 million
workers who are currently unemployed.

2. In the United States each year about 50,000 people are killed
in automobile accidents, and hundreds of thousands are seriously injured. It would be very desirable to decrease these
figures by a factor of two or more.

3. A city has 200 acres of land and 80 million dollars. The resi-
dents want a dome stadium designed for football, baseball,
basketball and soccer with movable seating to fit each sport.
Design the building.

These problem situations have several characteristics in common. Each involves numbers. Each has a description of an initial
or given situation. Each has a goal or some indication of a desired final situation. None can be solved by simple arithmetic
calculations. Indeed, each is a large and difficult problem with
no obvious or easy solution. They are typical of the real world
problems faced by people in business and government.

EXAMPLES OF PROBLEMS

1. Give an example of each of the following.

a. An arithmetic calculation
problem that can easily be
done mentally.

b. A fraction problem that
most people would solve
using pencil and paper.

c. An arithmetic calculation
where a calculator is a useful tool.

d. A geometry problem (one,
two, or three dimensional).

e. A story (word) problem.

2. Give examples of problems that people need to solve each
day at home or at their job.

3. Give an example of problems that people encounter in these areas.

    a. music   e. health
    b. art   f. social studies
    c. writing   g. physical education
    d. science   h. shop or home economics

4. Give an example of a social or phychological problem.

5. Give an example of a city planning or governmental problem.

DEFINING A PROBLEM

By now you should have a good idea of what a problem is.

The givens and goals are the most obvious parts of a problem. The third part is often not stated or obvious. It is the set of restrictions—or what is allowed in solving the problem.

Think about restrictions on math problems you solve in school.

Restrictions in taking a test.   Restrictions in homework.

   Do your own work.   Show all computation.

   Do not copy neighbor's   Use calculators only to
   paper.   check answers.

Remember the auto deaths problem several pages back? The goal is to cut auto deaths in half. But no restrictions are stated. Think about some steps that could be part of a solution. We could:

    a. ban driving on odd-numbered days.
    b. reduce the speed limit from 90 to 70 km per hour.
    c. not allow any driving after dark or on weekends.

How would voters react to those solutions? "Real world" problems are tricky because restrictions are usually not stated. It's hard to work within restrictions when they are not stated!

PARTS OF A PROBLEM

In many problem solving situations, the *givens, restrictions*, and *goals* are not clearly stated. Thus it is up to you to figure them out. If you cannot do this, the problem may not be well enough defined for you to solve. Your first task then becomes one of trying to get a more clear statement of the problem.

1. What part(s) (given, restriction, goal) seem to be missing in the following "problems"?

   a. 97.63
      2.57
      ‾‾‾‾

   b.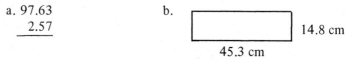
      45.3 cm

   c. I have a headache. What can I do to make it go away?

   d. The problem is that there is too much unhappiness in the world.

   e. Taxes are too high!

2. The planet Earth has a population of more than 4 billion and each year there are about 80 million *more* to feed. Half of the population is uderfed, and thousands die of malnutrition each day. World leaders would like to have no one starve or be malnourished.

   Make a list of restrictions for this problem. Do world leaders have to agree on the restrictions before they can try to solve the problem?

3. Identify the *givens, restrictions,* and *goals* in each problem situation below. If they are all present, solve the problem.

   a. The great detective Columbo found this scrap of paper when raiding the headquarters of a secret organization. He knows they had fewer than 20 members. The dues are a whole number of dollars and each member pays the same amount. If Columbo caught 5 in the raid, how many members do they still need to find?

b. Stingy Sharon wants to buy a motorcycle. She sees one priced at $1000. The next week it is priced at $500. The week after that, it is priced at $250. She buys it the following week. What does she pay? Do you know that for sure?

4. Design some calculator keyboards.

a. First make one that would be inconvenient to use. Lay it out in a ridiculous fashion.

b. You have been recently hired to design a keyboard for a calculator company. Design a convenient keyboard.

c. What features do you think calculators should have? Why?

PRIMITIVES

There are some problems that you can solve immediately because they are easy for you. Their solutions require little thinking. We will call these problems *primitives* or *simple exercises*.

Each of us has many primitives. Some of yours are the same as other people's primitives, while some are different. Finding 4 × 3 is easy for a 15-year-old student, but much harder for a 4-year-old child. Playing a major scale on a piano is very easy for a musician but not for a person untrained in music.

The idea of a primitive is very important. Schools try to teach a common core of primitives. Teachers can then use them to explain new ideas. One method of solving a hard problem is to break it down into smaller and easier problems. These problems may be ones you know how to solve – that is – primitives.

A calculator makes some problems into primitives. If your calculator has a square root key, a square root problem is a primitive for you, provided your calculator is available and working. Other function keys on a calculator (%, sin, 1/x, . . .)

help solve particular problems. People who understand the problem and have such a calculator to use add to their storehouse of primitives.

This is a very important idea. A problem can be a primitive because we have studied it very carefully and practiced solving it many times. Or, a problem can be a primitive because we have access to a machine that will solve it. For certain problems, access to a machine is an alternative to lots of training and experience.

PRIMITIVES FOR YOU

Consider a primitive to be a simple exercise, a problem you can solve easily and quickly. Answer these questions about primitives.

1. Make a list of all of your mental arithmetic primitives. These are calculations you can do mentally, quickly, and accurately.
   Examples:

   1 digit addition facts (3 + 5)
   1 digit multiplication facts (4 × 3)

2. List some geometry and/or measurement primitives you can do mentally.
   Examples:

   recognize polygons
   find areas of rectangles and squares

3. Using paper and pencil as a tool allows you to have more primitives. Longer problems are possible, such as column addition or multiplying two and three digit numbers. Make a list of primitives you have with pencil and paper.

4. List some geometry primitives when you are allowed to use tools such as a ruler, compass, protractor.

   Example:

   > measure line segments to nearest cm.
   > construct a square with sides of length 10 cm.

5. Is the process of checking answers in long division a primitive for you? Work the problem 7232 ÷ 16 and check it, using paper and pencil.

6. Work the same problem on your calculator. Do you have more confidence in your calculator answer or in your paper and pencil answer? Which method is faster and easier for you? If a calculation is done on a calculator, do you still need to check the answer?

7. Is long division with decimals a primitive for you when:

   > Using pencil and paper?
   > Using a calculator?
   > Which tool would you rather use?

8. All calculators have keys for +, ×, ÷, −. Does your calculator have other function keys? If so, make a list of them. Then try to make up a problem for each of these keys. If you understand the problems and meanings of the functions, these problems are primitives for you.

9. Have you had any formal training in music or sports? If so, name some of your primitives in one of those areas. Repeat the exercise for home economics, art, or crafts.

STEPS IN PROBLEM SOLVING

George buys six dozen eggs at 78 cents per dozen. How much does he pay? Is this an addition, subtraction, multiplication, or division problem? Knowing *when* to multiply is as important as knowing *how* to multiply.

Most books about problem solving list four major steps. All steps require thinking, and all can involve calculation. But the main amount of calculation is apt to occur in the third step.

> 1. Understand the problem
> 2. Devise a plan
> 3. Carry out the plan
> 4. Look back

Try the four steps on this problem:

A. *Understand the problem*

Read it carefully. Restate the problem in your own words. Look for the *givens* and the *goals*. Are *restrictions* stated? How can you tell when you have found a solution? Is five pennies, a nickel, a dime, a quarter, and a half dollar a solution?

B. *Devise a plan*

Books on problem solving list and discuss a number of general purpose plans. These plans can be used on lots of different problems. Some examples include:

Make a chart.

Look for a pattern.

Work backwards.

Guess and check.

Break into smaller problems.

1¢	5¢	10¢	25¢	50¢

These rows and columns will be used to systematically list all possible cases

Often two or more of these are used together. We will try guess and check and make use of a chart to keep track of our results. We will also break the problem down into simpler problems.

C. *Carry out the plan*

Can there be any solutions with exactly one penny? With exactly two pennies? How about the five penny case? How about solutions with no pennies? This is a (slightly) simpler problem from the original. Are eight or nine nickels a possibility? How about six or seven nickels?

1¢	5¢	10¢	25¢	50¢
5				
This leaves four coins to make 95¢				

1¢	5¢	10¢	25¢	50¢
	7	Two coins needed for 65¢		
	6	Three coins needed for 70¢		

D. *Look back*

Do the results make sense? Have all the solutions been found? (By now you should have found two solutions. Keep working — there are some more.)

PRACTICE THE STEPS

Practice the four general steps in problem solving on this problem:

What is the remainder when 5^{999} is divided by 7?

1. *Understand the problem.*

Restate it here in your own words.

To show that you understand the problem, solve a simpler problem: the remainder of $5^2 \div 7$.

2. *Devise a plan.*

Write it down.

Hint: Examine simpler cases to look for a pattern.

$5^1 \div 7 = 5 \div 7 = \underline{0} \text{rem} \underline{5}$

$5^2 \div 7 = 25 \div 7 = \underline{3} \text{rem} \underline{4}$

$5^3 \div 7 =$

$5^4 \div 7 =$

3. *Carry out the plan.*

Extend the chart and look for a pattern.

4. *Look back.*

Does the answer make sense?
Is there some way of checking your answer?
Can the problem be solved in another way?

PROBLEMS TO SOLVE

Use the four steps to solve these problems.

1. How many degrees are there in a 20-sided polygon?
   Hint: A triangle has 180°.

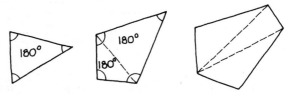

2. To number the pages of a thick book, the printer used 2989 digits, starting at page one. How many pages were in the book?

3. There were 18 people at a party. Someone suggested that each person shake hands once with every other person there. How many handshakes were there?

4. A group of people leave a party at the same time. They find the seventh floor elevator to take them down to the lobby. They get into the elevator one at a time. When the last person gets on, the bell rings and the door stays open. How many

people are on the elevator? What do you need to know to
solve this problem? Estimate this information and solve the
problem.

5. The general plan you developed to solve the 5^{999} problem
can be used on similar problems. Try it on the following.
   Find the remainder when 7^{1000} is divided by 5.
   Find the remainder when 9^{500} is divided by 7.

GUESS AND CHECK

Devising a plan for solving a problem is not an easy step.
There are many different methods to choose from.

Have you ever tried a method called Guess and Check? It's
also called trial and error. It is useful in problems where one can
tell if a correct answer has been found. For example:

Find a number such that

$\square^2 - 3 \times \square = 238$

Here is the way one person worked to solve it.

1st guess $\boxed{10}$ Check: Does $\boxed{10}^2 - 3 \times \boxed{10} = 238?$

$100 - \quad 30 \quad = \quad 70?$

too small!

So try a larger guess:

2nd guess $\boxed{20}$ Check: Does $\boxed{20}^2 - 3 \times \boxed{20} = 238?$

$400 - \quad 60 \quad = 340?$

too large!

What would your next guess be?

3rd guess $\square$ Check: Does $\square^2 - 3 \times \square = 238?$

Finish solving this problem. When the guess and check process involves many calculations, a calculator is a useful tool.
Show your guesses and checks in these problems.

1. a. $\square^2 - 3 \times \square = 238$
   b. $\square^2 + 8 \times \square = 945$
   c. $\square^3 + \square^2 + \square = 7.125$

2. Find negative numbers that are solutions for problems 1a and
1b.

3. Find a positive number N (accurate to 2 decimal places) such that

$$(\square \times \square) + \square = 100$$

TRY GUESSING

1. Work these problems on your calculator:

   $142^2 =$ Observe that the answer is a 5-digit number

   $785^2 =$ Observe that the answer is a 6-digit number.

   Now try some more problems involving 3-digit numbers. Show the details of your work to *prove* your answer is correct.

   a. Can the square of a 3-digit number be less than 5 digits in length?

   b. Can the square of a 3-digit number be more then 6 digits in length?

   c. What is the largest 3-digit number whose square is a 5-digit number?

   d. Find the smallest 3-digit number shose square is a 6-digit number?

2. You have a quadrilateral (4-sided polygon) with a perimeter of 18 cm. What quandrilateral will give you the largest area if the sides are whole numbers?

   What will the shape be if the sides do not have to be whole numbers?

3.   S E N D   The problem at the left involves an addition
    + M O R E   of two numbers. Each letter stands for a dif-
                       ferent digit. Match the digits and letters.

4. Farmer Frannie raises turkeys and rabbits. One day she noticed her animals had 50 heads and 140 feet. How many turkeys and rabbits does she have?

   Hint:

	Turkeys (2 feet)	Rabbits (4 feet)	Feet (total)
	50	0	100
	0	50	200

   Continue guessing until you have it solved.

5. If possible, find the number of turkeys and rabbits if there is a total of:
   a. 10 heads and 24 feet.   b. 20 heads and 55 feet.
6. Debbie and Diane start riding their bicycles toward each other from a distance 70 km apart. Debbie averages 12 km per hour and Diane averages 8 km per hour. How long will it take them to meet? Express the answer in minutes.
7. The sum of two numbers is 548. One number is 30 more than the other. What is the larger number?
8. Don says, "I have a number in mind. If you double it, then add 56, the sum is 400. What is my number?

METHODS OF CALCULATION

Calculation *is* important in solving math problems. People have worked for many years to develop good methods of calculating, and to develop aids for calculating. The *abacus* was a very early aid to calculations; historians have traced early forms of the abacus back about 5,000 years.

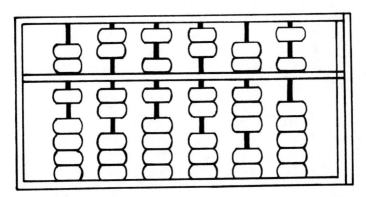

Our number system itself is an important aid to calculation. The languages of some primitive people contain only number words for "one", "two", "three", and "many". Children in these cultures do not learn how to count to ten or how to add simple numbers like three and two.

LV/ MMDXLV   The Roman Numeral System represented progress but was hard to work with. Try the long division problem given at the left.

The first machine that could add, subtract, multiply, and divide was developed by Wilhelm Schickard in 1623. Blaise Pascal (1642) and Gottfried Leibniz (1671) are also known for their work on building early calculators. By 1820 people knew how to build quite good calculators, and they were available for sale in stores.

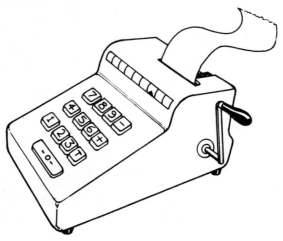

Work on a computer was begun by Charles Babbage in England during the 1820's, but that was a long time before we had vacuum tubes or other modern electrical equipment. Thus he failed, and it wasn't until 1945 that the first general purpose electronic digital computer was completed and used.

People now use a variety of methods and aids in calculation. A list of common ones is given below.

1. *Mental arithmetic.* Most people memorize the 1-digit addition and multiplication facts. They learn to mentally do simple calculations rapidly and accurately. About three-fourths of all calculations that people encounter in their everyday lives can be done mentally.

2. *Math tables.* You have probably used a "times" table to look up the product of two numbers. Suppose that doughnuts are 17 cents each, or $1.95 per dozen. Then the table below gives the price of any number of doughnuts up to three dozen and 11.

Doz.	*Number of additional doughnuts*											
	0	1	2	3	4	5	6	7	8	9	10	11
0	0	.17	.34	.51	.68	.85	1.02	1.19	1.36	1.53	1.70	1.87
1	1.95	2.12	2.29	2.46	2.63	2.80	2.97	3.14	3.31	3.48	3.65	3.82
2	3.90	4.07	4.24	4.41	4.58	4.75	4.92	5.09	5.26	5.43	5.60	5.77
3	5.85	6.02	6.19	6.36	6.53	6.70	6.87	7.04	7.21	7.38	7.55	7.72

3. *Pencil and paper.* Currently our schools place great emphasis on this. All students are expected to learn pencil and paper methods for addition, subtraction, multiplication, and division of whole numbers, decimal fractions, and fractions.

4. *Calculators.* Although calculating machines have been available for hundreds of years, it is only recently that they became very cheap. Now almost every home and business in the United States has a calculator.

5. *Computers.* The cost of computers has decreased very rapidly in recent years. Computers are common in large and small businesses and are starting to appear in homes and schools.

DO SOME CALCULATIONS

Which of the five methods you use depends upon the particular situation. You should have knowledge and skill in each of the methods and should begin to learn when each method is most appropriate.

Remember that while the calculation is an important step, one must work at understanding problems as well. Recognizing

the method to use and what a reasonable answer will be makes
you a better problem solver.

1. Think back over the past 24 hours. Did you do any pencil
   and paper arithmetic during this time? If so, when? Did you
   do any mental arithmetic? Give examples of when.

2. Add one more row to the doughnut price table. Then use the
   doughnut price table to find the price of the following number of doughnuts.

   a. 8   b. 4 dozen
   c. 1 dozen and 5   d. 50

   Many people can mentally calculate that 50 X $.17 = $8.50.
   Explain why this is not the correct cost of 50 doughnuts.

3. The price of doughnuts increases to $2.19 per dozen and 19
   cents apiece. Make a table that gives the price of any number
   of doughnuts up to three dozen. What will the cost of 100
   doughnuts be?

4. The price of doughnuts increases to 20 cents apiece, or $2.40
   per dozen. Solve problems 2a – 2d mentally using these prices.

TIME YOURSELF

Here are two groups of 20 number fact problems. Do the first
group *mentally*. Work rapidly but carefully. Record your time
and number of errors.

5 + 3 =	6 − 2 =	8 X 2 =	5 ÷ 5 =
2 + 8 =	8 − 3 =	3 X 8 =	24 ÷ 8 =
10 + 5 =	10 − 6 =	4 X 4 =	7 ÷ 1 =
3 + 9 =	13 − 9 =	6 X 5 =	32 ÷ 4 =
12 + 5 =	15 − 7 =	9 X 4 =	56 ÷ 7 =

Do this group using a calculator. Key in *each calculation* and
record the calculator answer. Give your time and number of
errors.

7 + 2 =	9 − 3 =	7 X 3 =	8 ÷ 2 =
9 + 4 =	7 − 5 =	4 X 6 =	25 ÷ 5 =
10 + 7 =	10 − 4 =	2 X 9 =	63 ÷ 9 =

$3 + 6 =$	$14 - 8 =$	$5 \times 7 =$	$42 \div 7 =$
$11 + 5 =$	$16 - 8 =$	$8 \times 8 =$	$54 \div 9 =$

What conclusion can you draw from this experiment?

BEST METHOD?

Here are some calculation problems. Decide which method *you* would use to solve them. Label the problem with

M mental arithmetic   *P* paper and pencil   *C* calculator

Work rapidly — you are not being asked to do the calculations.

1. ☐ $\begin{array}{r} 6 \\ \times 9 \\ \hline \end{array}$

2. ☐ $\begin{array}{r} 13 \\ 28 \\ + 12 \\ \hline \end{array}$

3. ☐ $\dfrac{84.48}{4} =$

4. ☐ $\begin{array}{r} 63.9 \\ \times 18.7 \\ \hline \end{array}$

5. ☐ $\begin{array}{r} 7843 \\ -3521 \\ \hline \end{array}$

6. ☐ $\begin{array}{r} 7.91 \\ 87.2 \\ +635. \\ \hline \end{array}$

7. ☐ $9 + 6 + 8 + 2$

8. ☐ $3 \times 5 \times 2 \times 4$

9. ☐ 821×1000

10. ☐ $13 \times 13 \times 13$

11. ☐ $\sqrt{16}$

12. ☐ $\sqrt{17}$

13. ☐ $(8 \times 7) - 4^2$

14. ☐ $\dfrac{63.63}{21}$

15. ☐ $\dfrac{17.8^2}{17.8}$

16. ☐ $\dfrac{16.4 \times 22.9}{135}$

17. ☐ $76 + 24$

18. ☐ $81 + 19 - 20 + 15$

19. ☐ $5\overline{)936}$

20. ☐ $\begin{array}{r} 1000 \\ + 900 \\ \hline \end{array}$

CHALLENGE PROBLEMS

1. What is the largest number that can be multiplied by itself without producing an overflow (a number too large to fit) on

the calculator display. First write down your general plan of attack and then solve it.

2. Suppose you have a clock that will run for exactly 100,000 seconds if it is fully wound up. You wind the clock fully, noting that it is exactly 12:00 noon on a Monday. What time (what day, and will it be AM or PM) will it be when the clock stops?

3. Find the patterns in these pairs of problems.

48	84	64	46	39	93	12	21
X21	X12	X23	X32	X31	X13	X63	X36

Make up some pairs that produce the same results.

4. A person's heart beats about 72 times per minute. If the person lives to be 75 years old, approximately how many times has his/her heart beaten?

5. What is the date when a year (not a leap year) is 200,000 minutes old? (Hint: The problem is to convert 200,000 minutes to days and to figure out the resulting date. The figure below might help.)

Month	J	F	M	A	M	J	J	A	S	O	N	D
Days	31	28										

First write down the plan of attack and then carry it out.

GETTING RIGHT ANSWERS

CALCULATOR ERRORS

It would be nice to always get the right answer in a calculation, but even using a calculator will not make this happen. There are too many things that can go wrong. Here are some of them.

1. An error in reading the numbers of the operations.

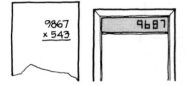

2. An error in directions given to the calculator (like the order of operations).

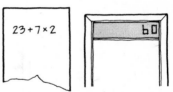

How can you get the right answer of 37?

3. A keyboarding error, such as double keying.

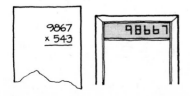

4. An error caused by the calculator not working right (caused by low batteries, dropping the machine, or extreme temperatures).

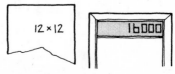

5. An error in reading or writing down the calculator answer.

As you can see, using a calculator does not guarantee right answers. There are ways to avoid and detect calculator errors. These methods, like the general problem solving steps, become easier with practice.

A VISUAL CHECK

Five sources of calculator errors were given in the previous section. Three of them are easily avoided. These are the reading (1), keying (3), and writing (5) errors. To avoid them, remember to look and think very carefully before, during, and after the calculation.

Use your calculator to find the product of 82953 and 681. Key in the first number and look at the display.

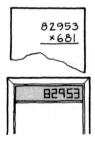

Do a *visual* check, comparing each digit carefully. A small keying error (such as reversing two digits) will give you a wrong answer.

Next key in the operation X. Since the display for a pocket calculator does not display the operation, there is no way to do

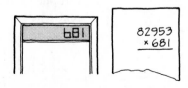

a visual check. Pushing the wrong operation key is a harder error to detect.

Key in the second number, (681). Check it visually.

Finally push the = key and check the answer displayed. Compare it to what you *expected* it to be. A rough mental estimate can be used to detect obvious errors. For example, you can detect whether you accidently pushed the + key instead of the X key.

The last step is copying, or using, your answer from the display. Do so carefully with another visual check.

WHAT DO YOU CALL A SOFT LEAD PENCIL?

To answer the question, try these calculator exercises. Write the letter of each exercise above its answer. If the message works, you probably got the right answers. If you made errors, try to find what caused them and rework the calculations.

E $57 \div 3 \times 17 - 40$

A $63570 \div 65$

N 300×1.62

B $25200 \div 720$

C $1.7 + 8 \times 7.9$

O $18^2 + 15^2$

M $40(32 - 1.7)$

R $2^6 \times 2^4$

W $5/16$

D one tenth minus one thousandth

L 35% of 6

T $32 - 4.5 \times 8 + 50$

U $(8.3 + 7.7)^3 - 3196$

$$\overline{\quad 978 \quad}$$

$$\overline{486} \quad \overline{900} \quad \overline{1212} \quad \overline{35} \quad \overline{283} \quad \overline{1024}$$

$$\overline{549} \quad \overline{486} \quad \overline{283}$$

$$\overline{.3125} \quad \overline{549} \quad \overline{549} \quad \overline{.099} \quad \overline{283} \quad \overline{486}$$

$$\overline{64.9} \quad \overline{978} \quad \overline{2.1} \quad \overline{64.9} \quad \overline{900} \quad \overline{2.1} \quad \overline{978} \quad \overline{46} \quad \overline{549} \quad \overline{1024}$$

TWICE OVER

One very good way to check an answer is to do the calculation over again. If possible, do it in a different order.

```
 8397        576
  235       6721
 6721        235
+ 576      +8397
```

Do these pairs of calculations. They show how to do addition and multiplication calculations in a different order.

$$82953 \times 681 = \qquad 681 \times 82953 =$$

If you get the same answer twice, you assume that it is the right answer. How is it still possible to get a wrong answer?

The process of reversing the order illustrates the commutative property for addition and multiplication. Is it possible to use the property for subtraction and division?

$$30 \div 6 = 5 \qquad 6 \div 30 = .2 \quad 13 - 7 = 6 \quad 7 - 13 = -6$$

The answer is no. Subtraction and division do not follow a commutative rule. But one can work a subtraction problem in the reverse order. Try these:

```
  1937        -639
-  639       +1937
```
$$8174 - 6295 = -6295 + 8174$$

One has to use care to avoid an error in checking a calculation. A student keys in: $1937 - 639 =$ and gets 1298.

To check this answer the student then continues by keying $-639 + 1937 =$ and gets 2596. Something is wrong! What is the problem? Experiment with your calculator, using smaller numbers, until you understand the difficulty here.

One cannot change the order around in a division calculation and expect to get the same answer. So if you want to check a division problem, one way is to just do the original calculation twice. Make sure you select the right order. For example, what is $67\overline{)59831}$? Is it $67 \div 59831$ or $59831 \div 67$?

To avoid this error, use a quick mental check. Should the answer be larger than 1 or smaller than 1? You can see (mentally) that the asnwer to the example should be larger than 1. Dividing in the wrong order produces an answer smaller than 1.

CHECK YOUR ANSWERS

Use a calculator to do and check these exercises.

For each of these problems, show the first calculator answer. Then rewrite the problem by changing the order, and then calculate its answer. Compare the two answers.

1.   9876   4. $389 + 43 + 165 + 7 =$
        5843
       16573
     + 48256   5. $1288 \times 258 \times 56 =$

2.   94.5
     $\times$ 892   6. $957,621 - 5637 =$

3.   1678   7. $89 - 43 - 65 + 127 - 36 =$
     $-$ 989

Study these division problems and estimate an answer.

Mark it as $<$ (less than 1)

               $=$ (equal to 1)

               $>$ (greater than 1)

Work the problems and write in your answer.

8.   5888889/9   10. $60864 \div 634$

9. $.219 \div 12.7313$ 11. How many times does
                                  27 go into 2646?

WORKING BACKWARDS

Calculate

$$
\begin{array}{r}
3974 \\
- 2895 \\
\hline
1079 \quad \text{Answer}
\end{array}
$$

3974 Check by adding

A subtraction calculation can be checked by addition. That is because the operations of addition and subtraction are the inverses of each other. Similarly, the operations of multiplication and division are the inverses of each other. All four types of calculation can be checked by using inverses or working backwards and "undoing" the calculation.

Carry out these calculations.

Exercise	Answer	Check Process	
8946 + 593 =		−593 =	
79315 − 9876 =		+9876 =	
82953 × 681 =		÷ 681 =	
55543 ÷ 829 =		× 829	

Sometimes a calculation will not check exactly when using a calculator. This is caused by the 8-digit accuracy in the calculation. For example:

$$4 \div 3 = \boxed{1.3333333} \qquad \times 3 = \boxed{3.9999999}$$

We know that $4 \div 3$ gives the repeating decimal 1.3333333.... Most calculators get and display the first 8 digits, so when the calculator answer is multiplied by 3, the result is 3.9999999. This is very close to 4, so the answer "checks".

Carry out these calculations, filling in all the missing boxes. Use the checking ideas given previously.

$89.5 \div 5.6 = \boxed{} \times \boxed{} = \boxed{}$

$123.4567 \times 987.654 = \boxed{} \div \boxed{} = \boxed{}$

$97382.374 - 27.927846 = \boxed{} + \boxed{} = \boxed{}$

$617.31928 + 974672.35 = \boxed{} - \boxed{} = \boxed{}$

Do each of the following exercises. Write down the "checking backwards" calculation, then show the results of checking each calculation by working backwards.

1. 287 X 9316

2. 389.4 X .76

3. 1288 + 258

4. 97532 − 8297

5. 1222155 ÷ 99.1

6. 80092.4 ÷ 428.3

7. 89735.6 − 2.81794

8. 12345678 + .12345

9. 1894 − 695 + 781 − 674

10. 1894 ÷ 12 X 37

USE YOUR HEAD

One way to avoid calculator errors is not to use a calculator! A machine is not needed for some of the number fact primitives. You should be able to do these facts mentally, with no errors.

Other calculations can be figured out mentally, though you need not memorize the answer. In "the good old days" students received a lot of instruction on mental arithmetic. Given below are a number of examples from an 1897 math book.*

---

* *Commercial Progressive Arithmetic* by Wallace H. Whigam and Samuel H. Goodyear. Goodyear-Marshall Publishing Co., 1903. Examples on following pages are from this textbook.

Adding single columns

Try these:

In adding orally a series of numbers, simply announce results; do not say "5 and 7 are 12 and 5 are 17", etc.; say "5, 12, 17", etc.

5	3	8
7	6	1
5	2	6
3	8	3
6	4	5
+ 3	9	2
	+ 6	7
		+ 4

Add rapidly and with certainty, and allow nothing to divert the attention until the result is obtained. After recording the final result, verify by adding the problem again, beginning at the other end.

Subtracting numbers

In subtracting numbers, knowing their 'complements' may prove helpful. The ability to do this is very useful in making change.

6 and 4 7 and 3	27 and 43 42 and 58	364 and 636
Make 10	Make 100	Make 1000

Name as rapidly as you can the complements of the following numbers. The sum of the given number and your answer should be an appropriate power of 10.

8	3	92	749
55	87	263	80

Find the change required by subtracting mentally the sum of the items from the amount paid. (No tax is involved.)

Items	Paid	Items	Paid
1. 15¢, 19¢, 50¢	$1.00	3. $3.25, 50¢, $1.25	$ 5.00
2. 45¢, 55¢, 98¢	$2.00	4. $4.60, $2.25, $1.20	$10.00

Multiplying

3 X 9 = 27	3 X 12 = 36	3 X 16 =
3 X 10 = 30	3 X 13 =	3 X 30 =
3 X 11 = 33	3 X 14 =	3 X 35 =

To multiply some numbers in your head, extend the multiplication table that you already know.

Write down the answers you can arrive at mentally.

1. 15 X 6 =

2. 19 X 2 =

3. 24 X 3 =

4. 17 X 4 =

5. 3 X 28 =

6. 6 X 14 =

7. 4 X 25 =

8. 350 X 2 =

9. 1900 X 4 =

10 18 X 30 =

11. 2800 X 3 =

12. 470 X 2 =

13. What will 3 books cost at $.75 each?

14. The 1897 graduating class attends a theatre performance where the tickets are $.25 each. What is the cost for all 30 seniors?

15. At 20 cents an hour, what can a person earn in 3 days of 8 hours each?

Short division

Short division is an abbreviated form in which the various multiplications and subtractions are performed mentally. It is used when the divisor number is small.

$$7\overline{)2552} \quad 364 \text{ rem } 4$$

Explanation: 7 is contained in 25, 3 times, with 4 remaining, we write the 3 as the first digit of the quotient, and *mentally prefix* the 4 to the next figure, which gives 45 as the dividend in the next step, and so on.

Give results *at sight* of the divisions here indicated.

1. 3⟌45

2. 13⟌42

3. 16⟌80

4. 7⟌24

5. 18⟌72

6. 3⟌53

7. 9⟌1000

8. 7⟌1008

9. 4⟌580

10. At $.02 each, how many apples can be bought for $1.75?

Combinations: Write answers to those you can do *mentally*.

1. From 3 hours subtract 1¼ hours.

2. A house rents for $40 per month. What is the rent for:

          1/4 month   5/8 month?

3. At 30¢ each, how many music books can be bought for $6.30?

4. 8 days is what part of 8 weeks?

5. Henry earned $45 in 15 days; what did he earn in a day?

6. Sara stayed at an inn for 5 days and paid 3½ dollars. How much is that per day?

7. $(17 - 8) \div 3 =$

8. $(51 \div 17) + 9 - (2 \times 4)$

9. $\dfrac{(75 \div 15) + 9}{2} =$

10. $\dfrac{(25 - 6) \times (52 \div 13)}{(3 \times 13) - 37}$

MORE TECHNIQUES

Mental calculations require a high degree of skill with the basic facts. The following two techniques may also be helpful to you.

Look For Patterns

1. $3 \times 10 = 30$ 5. $550 \div 10 = 55$

2. $35 \times 100 = 3500$ 6. $75000 \div 100 =$

3. $17 \times 1000 =$ 7. $50 \div 100 = .5$

4. $3.2 \times 100 =$ 8. $7 \div 1000 =$

Look at the Problem Differently

Think of 198 as $200 - 2$.

So $(200 - 2) \times 4 = 800 - 8 =$ ____

| 198×4 |

Practice on these:

1. $398 \times 6 =$ 3. $502 \times 6 =$

2. $22 \times 50 =$ 4. $1999 \times 3 =$

Use the above techniques to help solve the following problems.

1. Notice that $15^2 =$ 225   The last two digits of the answer

   $25^2 =$ 625   end in what numbers? How can

   $85^2 =$ 7225   you get the rest of the digits in

   $105^2 =$ 11025   in the answer?

Predict mentally and check with your calculator.

$$45^2 \qquad 55^2 \qquad 75^2 \qquad 95^2$$

2. What is the sum of the first 25 numbers? Use this to help you.

$$1 + 2 + 3 + 4 + \ldots + 22 + 23 + 24 + 25$$

3. Study the following examples.

   $17 \times 11 =$

   $17 \times 10 + 17 =$

   $170 + 17 = 187$

$$\begin{array}{r} 17 \\ \times 11 \\ \hline 17 \\ 17 \\ \hline 187 \end{array}$$

Solve the problems below mentally and check with a calculator.

$$23 \times 11 \qquad 52 \times 11 \qquad 86 \times 11 \qquad 74 \times 11$$

APPROXIMATE MENTAL ARITHMETIC

Mental arithmetic can give the exact answer to many problems. What is 3.5×10? You shouldn't need a calculator for this.

Often one does not need an exact answer. *Approximate* mental arithmetic may solve the problem. You are driving at 85 km/hr and see a road sign saying 200 km to your destination. You wonder how long it will take you to get there. You think to yourself:

1 hour for 85 km

2 hours for 170 km

That leaves 30 km to go.

The 30 km will take 30/85 of an hour.

That is more than $\frac{1}{3}$ of an hour but less than $\frac{1}{2}$ of an hour.

Thus mental arithmetic gives an answer of about $2\frac{1}{3}$ to $2\frac{1}{2}$ hours.

Mental arithmetic is very useful in detecting errors made using a calculator. It is also useful as one thinks about a problem, trying to figure out how to solve it. Practice your mental approximation skills and they will get better.

Do a mental approximation to solve these problems. Then solve each one more exactly using a calculator. If your mental answer is a lot different from your calculator answer, check it again. Either could be in error.

1. You have just taken off from Los Angeles to fly to New York, a distance of 5200 km. Your pilot announces that your ground speed is 970 km/hr. How long will it take you to get there?

2. You buy items at a grocery store costing 79¢, $1.19, $2.50, and 49¢. What is the total bill?

3. A baseball player has 14 hits in 45 times at bat. What is his batting average?

MULTIPLICATION APPROXIMATIONS

You have a problem that involves the calculation of 53 × 421. You may decide to use a calculator or paper or pencil if you want an exact answer, but for a guess or judging the reasonableness of your exact answer, a mental calculation is appropriate.

53 × 421 is close to 50 × 400 or 20 0 00. That's 20 thousand

If you used the calculator for 53 × 421, you could accidently key in 533 × 421 or 53 × 21. How could this happen? Will mental approximation detect these errors?

Approximate these answers by working with first digits. Fill in with zeros to keep track of place value.

```
Exercise                                    0 0
                                            ↗ ↗ ↗ 0    Think 7×1
        58 → 50   or think        132 ↗          and attatch
      × 91 → 90   5 × 9 and      × 73            3 zeroes
                  attatch 2                      so → 7000
                  zeroes → 4500
```

We call this method *first digit approximation*.

1. Use first digit approximation to figure out which products
   are obviously wrong. Give your mental answer for each calculation. You may use a calculator to check your conclusions.

817	98	92615	98.2
X 31	X 97	X 41	X 3.84
254087	9506	3797215	3770.88

63.8	125	3.922	.37
X 985	X 6.7	X 875	X 9.5
62843	837.5	343.175	.3515

2. Use first digit approximations to solve these problems.

   a. A 216 page paperback book had an average of 350 words
      per page. How many words are in the book?

   b. Jan's typing rate is 55 words a minute. How many words
      can she type in an hour and a half?

DIVISION APPROXIMATIONS

First digit approximation can also be used in division problems.

8972 ÷ 27   In doing 8972 ÷ 27, you acci-
   ↓   First digits   dentally key in 89772 ÷ 27.
8000 ÷ 20   What did you get?
   ↓   Mental arithmetic   Explain how first digit approx-
 800 ÷ 2   imation detects this error.
   ↓   Mental arithmetic
400

First digit approximations are very crude. They will not
detect all possible division keying errors.

839 ÷ 468   Some possible keying errors are 839 ÷ 485
   ↓   or 893 ÷ 468.
800 ÷ 400   Calculate each of these, noting how close
   ↓   they are to the exact and approximate
2   answer.

The mental arithmetic in first digit division approximations is
sometimes not so easy.

8972 ÷ 37 → 8000 ÷ 30 → 800 ÷ 3   But what is that?

Think of it as $(8 \div 3) \times 100$. To the nearest whole number, 8/3 is 3. So the approximate answer is 300.

1. Do first digit approximations on the following.

$$\frac{9347}{32} \qquad \frac{6528}{24} \qquad \frac{97938}{3215} \qquad \frac{814}{32}$$

2. Some of the following calculations contain errors that can be detected by first digit approximation. Circle them.

$$\frac{37}{16} = 23.125 \qquad \frac{8295}{45} = 184.33333 \qquad \frac{671}{89} = .7547806$$

$$\frac{67}{325} = .2061538 \qquad \frac{929}{9874} = .9344744 \qquad \frac{36.5}{9.82} = 3.7169042$$

3. (Use first digit approximations.) You need to write a 4000 word paper. If you write about 300 words per hour, how long will it take?

ADDITION AND SUBTRACTION APPROXIMATIONS

First digit approximations can be used on addition and subtraction problems.

$$839 + 42 + 729 + 5 \ ?$$

Suppose we are faced with this problem. We observe that "hundreds" is the largest place value present. So we mentally do the following.

	Try this one:
$839 = 839 \to 800$	81473
$42 = 042 \to 000$	6283
$729 = 729 \to 700$	32947
$+ \ 5 = 005 \to 000$	742
$\overline{\qquad 1500}$	1659
	+28371

Similar ideas can be used in working with decimal numbers and in subtraction.

$$\begin{array}{rl}
\$47.95 \rightarrow & 40.00 \\
6.23 \rightarrow & 0.00 \\
82.40 \rightarrow & 80.00 \\
.57 \rightarrow & .00 \\
\hline
& \$120.00
\end{array}
\qquad
\begin{array}{rl}
+\ 2841 \rightarrow & +\ 2000 \\
-\ 65 \rightarrow & -\ 0000 \\
-\ 3941 \rightarrow & -\ 3000 \\
+\ 611 \rightarrow & +\ 0000 \\
\hline
& -\ 1000
\end{array}$$

1. Do the first three addition problems given above using your calculator. What relation or pattern do you find in the first digit approximations versus exact answers?

2.

Mo	Day	To	Pay.	Dep.	Bal. Forward
					532.00
Aug	1	Rent	225.⁰⁰		
"	2	Car Repair	108.⁵⁸		
"	3	Shopping Spree	325.⁰⁰		

Is Jan's checking account in good or bad shape?

3. Use first digit arithmetic to look for obvious errors.

$$\begin{array}{r}
3200 \\
29 \\
5618 \\
397 \\
+\ 8921 \\
\hline
25365
\end{array}$$

$\$11.29 + \$64.47 + .35 + \$3.41 = \$79.52$

$-35 + 63 + 22 - 81 - 15 = 46$

$82 \times 37 - 43 \times 21 = 62811$

$4181 - 321 \times 12 = 329$

ROUNDING

First digit approximations often are not very accurate. To be closer to the answer, try rounding each number in the calculation to the nearest correct first digit.

Study these examples.

$$\begin{array}{rl}
47.90 \rightarrow & 50 \\
+\ 9.213 \rightarrow & 10 \\
\hline
& 60
\end{array}
\quad
\begin{array}{rl}
2241.8 \rightarrow & 2000 \\
-\ 828.5 \rightarrow & 800 \\
\hline
& 1200
\end{array}
\quad
\frac{829}{37} \rightarrow \frac{800}{40} \downarrow 20
\quad
\begin{array}{rl}
98.5 \rightarrow & 100 \\
\times 8.7 \rightarrow & 9 \\
\hline
& 900
\end{array}$$

Rounded first digit approximations can be done almost as fast as straight first digit approximations. Try the first example using the straight first digit technique. Compare the answer to the rounded approximation. Which is closer to the exact answer?

First Digit Mental	Exact	Rounded Mental
40	57.113	60

Rounded estimates *usually* are closer to exact answers than the first digit estimates. But not always.

Different books and/or teachers teach different rounding rules. Circle the correct answers. Then check with your teacher to make sure the two of you agree on rounding rules.

$$650 \begin{cases} ? \to 600 \\ ? \\ \to 700 \end{cases} \quad 350 \begin{cases} ? \to 300 \\ ? \\ \to 400 \end{cases} \quad -650 \begin{cases} ? \to -700 \\ ? \\ \to -600 \end{cases}$$

Use rounding rules to mentally estimate answers to these problems. Then solve such problems using a calculator.

1. 824.6
   ×39.5

2. $\dfrac{1894}{17}$

3. 1895.2
   +1743.8

4. $\dfrac{279.3}{3142}$

5. 98.3
   × 6.7

6. −61.3
   + −48.9

FORMULAS

PROCEDURES

In Chapter 2 we discussed some general ideas of problem solving. The second stage of this process is to devise a plan. Sometimes a problem is so simple one can select a plan from memory, while at other times one will need to think out a sequence of steps. Some simple examples are given below.

Problem Solving
1. Understand the problem
2. Devise a plan
3. Carry out the plan
4. Look back

Apples are four pounds for a dollar. What will one pound cost? Procedure: Divide $\dfrac{\$1.00}{4} = 25$ cents per pound	Oranges are 29 cents per pound. How much will six pounds cost? Procedure: Multiply $.29 \times 6 = \$1.74$
A jar of instant coffee is $4.79, but you have a coupon good for a fifty cent discount. What is your actual cost? Procedure: Subtract $4.79 - \$.50 = \$4.29$	You purchase the pound of apples, the six pounds of oranges, and the jar of coffee. What is the total cost? Procedure: Add $.25 + \$1.74 + \$4.29 = \$6.28$

In this chapter we will use the words *procedure* and *plan* interchangeably. A procedure is a plan for solving a specific type of problem. One way to represent a procedure is by means of a formula. Thus most of this chapter is about understanding and using formulas.

Often it takes a sequence of steps to solve a problem. It takes careful thinking to decide upon the steps in a plan and to carry them out in the right order.

Corn is $1.00 per dozen ears. What will seven ears cost?

Step 1 What will one ear cost?

Procedure: Divide

$$\frac{\$1.00}{12} = \$.08333\ldots$$

Procedure: Increase to next higher cent.

$.08333... $.09

Step 2 What will seven ears cost?

Procedure: Multiply

$.09 × 7 = $.63

Notice that the first step involved two single procedures. Consider an alternative method of solution.

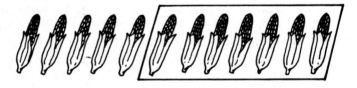

Seven ears = $\frac{7}{12}$ of a dozen

The cost is $\frac{7}{12}$ ($1.00) = .58333333

Increase to next higher cent. = .59

Is 63¢ or 59¢ the correct answer? Explain how correct mathematics can lead to two different answers to the same problem.

In each of the following problems first write down what procedure you will use. Then write down a mental estimate of the answer. Finally solve, using a calculator.

1. A baseball mitt costs $14.79, a ball costs $3.68, and a cap costs $2.49. What is the total cost of all three items?

2. Pat is paid $17.50 at the end of each week for the part-time job she has. If she saves all of it, how long will it take her to save enough money for a 10-speed bicycle costing $134.99?

3. Bagels are $2.08 per dozen, or 18 cents each. Orders of five dozen or more placed in advance receive a six percent discount. How much will 15 dozen bagels cost if ordered in advance? How much will 200 bagels cost if ordered in advance?

4. Corn is three cans for 79 cents and peas are four cans for 89 cents. What will be the total cost of one can of each?

5. A store is giving a 15% discount off the list price of each item. Terry buys a table listed at $87.40, two chairs listed at $26.90 each, and three pillows listed at $7.99 each. How much must Terry pay?

VARIABLES

Things about you change as you grow older. For example, your height and weight are values that vary over time. We call them variables.

A variable is something that has a name and a value, but whose value can vary. Variables are useful in expressing procedures.

Suppose you worked at a job that pays $2.65 an hour. For an eight hour day, your pay is $2.65 × 8 or $21.20. We could express your pay in words: *PAY = RATE × HOURS*. This formula shows how to figure your salary and it shows how the variables are related. *PAY, RATE*, and *HOURS* are all variables.

The distance you travel is determined by your rate (how fast you go) and your time (how long you go). It can be written: *DISTANCE = RATE × TIME*. To save writing, we can abbreviate the formula to D = R × T or D=RT (no sign between variables means they are multiplied together).

The distance across the U. S. is about 5000 km.

$$500 \text{ km} = 5 \frac{\text{km}}{\text{hr}} \times 1000 \text{ hrs}$$

$$= 80 \frac{\text{km}}{\text{hr}} \times 62.5 \text{ hrs}$$

$$= 1000 \frac{\text{km}}{\text{hr}} \times 5 \text{ hrs}$$

Which is the rate for flying? For walking? For driving?

Listed below are some common formulas. See if you can guess how these formulas are used, and the meaning of each variable.

$$A = \ell w \qquad I = prt \qquad P = 4s \qquad A = \tfrac{1}{2}bh \qquad C = \tfrac{5}{9}(F-32)$$

FORMULAS

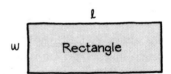

In the formula $A = \ell w$, A is a variable that stands for Area. ℓ stands for what variable name? w?

In $P = 2\ell + 2w$, the P means perimeter, and 2ℓ means 2 times the length.

1. Calculate the area and perimeter of each given rectangle.

	ℓ	w	*Area*	*Perimeter*
a	35 cm	20 cm		
b	89.4 cm	68.3 cm		
c	2.9 cm	17.8 cm		
d	3.6 cm	2.8 cm		

2. A square is a special kind of rectangle, whose length and width are the same. Let s be the variable name for the length of a side. Use the rectangle formulas or your memory to write formulas for the area and perimeter of a square.

   Find the area and perimeter of a square whose sides measure:

   a. 5.2 cm   b. 36 cm

3. Find the side of a square whose area is

   a. 361 cm²   b. 6.25 cm²

4. Find the total area of this rectangle. All shapes inside are squares.

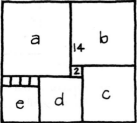

5. Find a square whose perimeter is equal to its area.

PICK'S LAW

Pick's Law is a formula that is helpful in finding areas of polygons. Suppose the polygon is made on a square grid, such as a geoboard. Find the area of Figure (a) by counting squares. It is easy to do that mentally, and get 7 square units. Now try Figure (b). It is harder, isn't it?

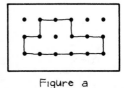

Figure a

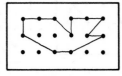

Figure b

Alfred Pick noticed a relationship between the outside and inside nails or dots in shapes like those pictured above. He expressed it this way.

$$A = \frac{O}{2} + I - 1$$

Area is equal to the number of 'on the side' nails divided by 2, added to the number of 'inside' nails minus 1. Check it with information from Figures (a) and (b).

$$A = \frac{14}{2} + 1 - 1$$

$$A = 7 + 1 - 1$$

$$A = 7 \text{ sq units}$$

$$A = \frac{12}{2} + 2 - 1$$

$$A = 6 + 2 - 1$$

$$A = 7 \text{ sq units}$$

Use Pick's law on these polygons to find their areas. Show your substitution process, but mentally calculate the answer.

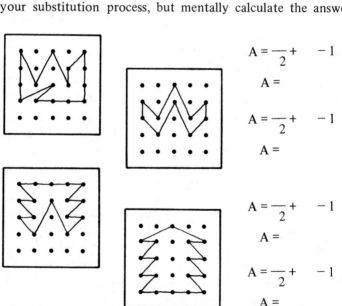

$$A = \frac{}{2} + \quad - 1$$

$$A =$$

$$A = \frac{}{2} + \quad - 1$$

$$A =$$

$$A = \frac{}{2} + \quad - 1$$

$$A =$$

$$A = \frac{}{2} + \quad - 1$$

$$A =$$

SEQUENCES

Formulas are useful in expressing the terms of a sequence.

4,   7,   10,   13,   16   (keep increasing by 3)

2,   4,   8,   16,   32   (keep doubling)

In the first example, a formula for the nth term is 3n+1. In the second, it is 2^n. Find the pattern and complete the following tables.

1	2	3	4	5	6	7	n
4	8	12					4n

1	2	3	4	5	6	7	n
3	6	9	12				

1	2	3	4	5	6	7	n
9	11	13					2n+7

1	2	3	4	5	6	7	n
15	18	21	24				

1	2	3	4	5	6	7	n
1	8	27	64				

1	2	3	4	5	6	7	8	9
5	7	11	19	35				

Sara talks her boss into this monthly salary: $1 for the first day, $2 for the second day, $4 for the third, and continuing to double each working day. What will she earn in the first ten days? Fill in the chart to find out. The two general formulas give you a daily salary and the total earned (n means the number of the day). Sara gets fired at the end of a month (20 working days). How much did she earn during that time?

Day	Salary	Total
1	$1	$1
2	$2	$3
3	$4	$7
4	$8	$15
5		
6		
7		
8		
9		
10		
n	2^{n-1}	$2^{n}-1$

MYSTIC ROSE

This geometric design is called a "mystic rose". It was produced by connecting every point on the circle to every other
point. How many different segments did the artist draw?

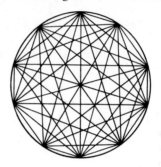

Connect the points on these circles and fill in the chart.

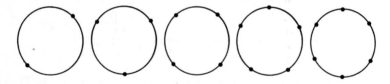

Points	Segments
1	1
2	3
3	6
4	
5	
6	
7	
8	
9	
10	
n	$\dfrac{n(n-1)}{2}$

Substitute numbers in the formula to check your work and
practice using the formula.

4 points (every 90°)	$\dfrac{\boxed{4}(\boxed{4}-1)}{2} = \dfrac{4(3)}{2} = 2 \times 3 = 6$

5 points
(every 72°) $\dfrac{\boxed{}(\boxed{}-1)}{2} = \dfrac{\boxed{}(\quad)}{2} =$

10 points (every 36°)	36 points (every 10°)
20 points (every 18°)	72 points (every 5°)

1. Suppose a graphic artist can draw a line connecting two dots in five seconds. About how long will it take the artist to draw a mystic rose with 10 points? At \$35 per hour, what will this cost?

The same formula can be used to determine the number of handshakes that can occur between a given number of people, when each person shakes hands with each other person *once*. For example, suppose six people attend a party and each shakes hands. There will be (6) × (5)/2 = 15 handshakes. Solve the problem for 10 people. For 100.

2. Suppose 200 people attend a large party and shake hands at the rate of one shake per three seconds. How long will it take to complete the handshaking if only one handshake occurs at a time? How long will it take if 200 handshakes occur at a time?

SUM A SEQUENCE

Many problems involve summing the terms of a sequence. Notice the dotted triangle. How many dots does it take to make a triangle whose sides are 20 dots in length?

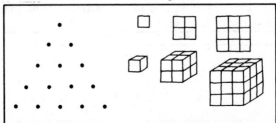

You can add up the number of dots in each row.

$1 + 2 + 3 + 4 + \ldots + 17 + 18 + 19 + 20$

One way to find this sum is to group the terms.

$1 + 20 = 21$ $2 + 19 = 21$ and so on with $10 + 11 = 21$

There are 10 pairs each summing to 21. The total sum is 210.

$$1 + 2 + 3 + \ldots + n = \frac{(n)(n+1)}{2}$$

Substitute: 20 for n

$$\frac{20(20+1)}{2} \text{ or } \frac{20 \times 21}{2}$$

What is the sum of the first 1000 counting numbers?

Use the pairing technique or revise the formula to find these sums:

$3 + 6 + 9 + 12 + \ldots + 300 =$

$2 + 7 + 12 + 17 + \ldots + 202 =$

$1^2 + 2^2 \cong 3$

$1^2 + 2^2 + 3^2 + \ldots + n^2 =$

$$\frac{(n)(n+1)(2n+1)}{6}$$

What is the sum of the first 1000 counting numbers?

A sheet of paper one metre square is cut into 1 cm squares. These are painted different colors and used to make a pattern containing a 1×1 square, a 2×2 square, a 3×3 square, etc. What is the largest square in the pattern? How many of the 1 cm squares are left over?

$$1^3 + 2^3 + 3^3 + \ldots + n^3 = \frac{[(n)(n+1)]^2}{2}$$

Test the formula for n = 1,2, and 3 to verify if it works. Find the sum for n = 10. For n = 100.

ARRANGEMENTS

How many different ways can Susan, Sara, Shawn, Sandy, and Sam pose in family pictures? The photographer wants all 5 together (a row of two and a row of three) but any of the children may sit in any of the chairs. This is a hard problem. A good way to attack it is to try a simpler problem.

How many different seating arrangements would there be for only 1 child?

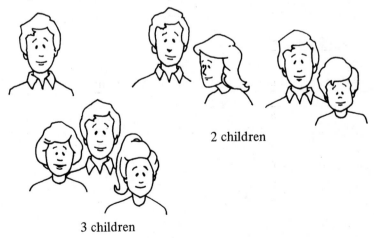

2 children

3 children

The photographer, after a *long* day, figured out the five children had tried 120 different seating arrangements.

Organize the information

Set up a chart

Look for a pattern

Number of objects	Number of arrangements	
1	1	
2	2	(2 × 1)
3	6	(3 × 2 × 1)
4	24	(4 × 3 × 2 × 1)
5	120	(5 × 4 × 3 × 2 × 1)
n	n!	n × (n−1) × . . . × 3 × 2 × 1

Note: Some calculators have a factorial key, labeled n!

Use your calculator

How many different seating arrangements are possible for the family portrait when the 2 parents join the five children?

How many different ways can the 9 Supreme Court Justices walk into the courtroom, if they enter single file?

How many different ways can the 11 members of a football team be introduced at the beginning of a televised game?

OH SAY CAN YOU SEE?

The formula

$$D = \sqrt{1.5\,h}$$

gives the distance (in miles) to the horizon. The h in the formula is the height in feet.

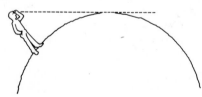

Example: A person at the top of a high building is 120 feet above ground level. How far can he see?

$$D = \sqrt{1.5 \times 120} \quad = \quad \sqrt{180} \quad = 13.4 \text{ miles}$$
    (substitute)   (multiply)   (find the square root)

1. A person is standing at sea level, with his eyes exactly five feet above the ground. How far away is the horizon for him?

2. A person is looking out the window at an airplane flying at 34,000 feet. It is a clear day and she can see the horizon far away. What is the distance she can see?

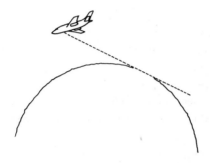

There is a similar formula using metric measurements, where h is in centimeters and the distance is in kilometers.

$$D = \sqrt{.126\,h}$$

3. The eyes of the person in Problem 1 above are 152.4 cm above sea level. Find the km distance of the horizon.

4. Terry is standing on a mountain that rises 2540 *meters* above ground level. Given a clear day, how far away can she see?

FALLING FORMULAS

The formula $D = 4.9t^2$ gives the distance (in meters) that an object will fall in t seconds. It assumes the fall is near the earth's surface and that there is little air resistance. That is, it assumes a dense object is falling. A feather is too light to be used in this formula.

Suppose a solid iron ball is dropped from a height of 300 m. How far will it fall in 1 second? (4.9 m)

3 seconds?

6 seconds?

How long will it take to reach the ground? (Find an answer to the nearest .5 second.)

The formula $V = 4.4\sqrt{d}$ gives the velocity in meters per second for an object that falls a distance of d meters. The falling iron ball will have a velocity of $4.4\sqrt{300} = 76.2$ meters per second when it hits the ground. Suppose the ball is dropped from a height of 150 m. What will its impact velocity be?

1. An iron ball is dropped from the top of Sears Tower in Chicago, which is 443 meters in height. What will its impact velocity be?

2. A baseball catcher attempts to field a "pop-up" which has risen to a height of 35 meters. What will the impact velocity be? (Assume a "belt-level" catch attempt, 1 meter above the ground.)

3. The high dive in Olympics is from a 10 meter high platform. If a diver rises 2 meters above the platform before beginning his downward descent, what will be his impact velocity?

4. A diver dives from the cliffs of Acupulco, Mexico, a height of about 40 meters. What will be the impact velocity? Calculate how long he will be airborn, to the nearest .5 second.

DISTANCE, RATE & TIME

A formula tells how two or more variables are related. Depending on the formula given, you can use it or variations of it to solve for different unknowns. Look at the formula $D = R \times T$. If any two of its variables are known, the third can be found.

Terry rides her bicycle 10 km per hour for 2 hours. How far does she go?

$D = R \times T$
$D = 10 \times 2$
$D = 20$ km

Terry bicycles 30 km in 2 hours. What is her rate of speed?

Rewrite: $R = D \div T$
$D = R \times T$ $R = 30 \div 2$
as $R = 15$ km/hr

Terry bicycles 40 km at the rate of 8 km/hr. How long does it take?

Rewrite: $T = D \div R$
$D = R \times T$ $T = 40 \div 8$
as $T = 5$ hrs

Find the missing values in the chart using your calculator and one of the formulas:

$$D = R \times T \qquad T = D \div R \qquad R = D \div T$$

	Distance	*Rate*	*Time*
a		55 km/hr.	7.5 hr.
b	972 cm	2 cm/sec.	
c	4800 km		6.25 hr.
d	32 km	8 m/sec.	

From *Ripley's Believe It or Not*

The distance record for walking on hands is probably still held by Johann Huslinger. In 1900 he walked from Vienna to Paris on his hands, going 10 hours each day for 55 days. If he averaged 1.53 km per hour, how many kms did he walk?

RELATED FORMULAS

We can use the area formula to write related formulas.

$$\ell = A/w \qquad w = A/\ell$$

If we need to find the width of the indicated rectangle, we can use the formula $w = A/\ell$. Thus the width is $100/20 = 5$ cm.

$\ell = 20$ cm

w $\quad A = 100$ cm^2

ℓ

w $\quad A = \ell w$
$\quad P = 2\ell + 2w$

Use the formula P = 2ℓ + 2w to write a formula for ℓ and a formula for w.

$$ℓ = \qquad w =$$

Find the missing values in the rectangle problems below. If you have trouble, draw a picture to help you, or make up a similar by easier problem and solve it first.

	Length	Width	Perimeter	Area
1	17 cm	13 cm		
2	144 cm			1728 cm²
3		15 cm		3250 cm²
4	19 cm		62 cm	
5		14.8	100 cm	
6			45.5 cm	98.6 cm²

7. A square has an area of 169 cm². What is its perimeter? A square has a perimeter of 5 km. What is its area?

THINK METRIC!

Temperatures on the Celsius and Fahrenheit scales are related by the formula

$$C = \tfrac{5}{9} (F-32)$$

This formula can be rewritten as

$$F = 32 + \tfrac{9}{5} C$$

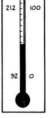

From the first formula one can see that 32° on the Fahrenheit scale is 0° (freezing temperature of water) on the Celsius scale. Use the second formula to see what 100° (boiling temperature of water) Celsius corresponds to on the Fahrenheit scale.

A radio station announced these nonmetric temperatures during the day. Calculate the Celsius temperatures.

1. 7 a.m.   48°F   3. 3 p.m.   86°F

2. 12 noon   70°F   4. 9 p.m.   65°F

The next day, you switch radio stations and this announcer gives Celsius temperatures. Find the Fahrenheit temperatures.

1. 7 a.m.   12°C   3. 3 p.m.   30°C

2. 12 noon   22°C   4. 9 p.m.   18°C

In linear measurement 1 inch = 2.54 cm. We can make a formula to convert inches to cm: cm = 2.54 × I. Estimate mentally (2.5 × inches), then calculate these lengths more accurately in cm.

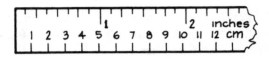

1. 4 inches   2. 6 inches   3. 12 inches   4. 36 inches

RIGHT TRIANGLES

Scientists and mathematicians have developed thousands of different formulas. A formula is a concise, shorthand method for representing a procedure. A formula tells you how to solve a particular type of problem.

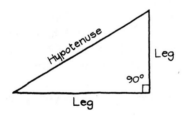

Geometry uses many interesting formulas. You have already used some of them for perimeter and area. Here we will study some formulas related to a right triangle.

Look at the right triangle pictured here. What two sides form the right angle? What side is opposite the right angle? A very old but useful formula was developed by a Greek mathematician named Pythagoras around the sixth century B. C. It has been called the Pythagorean Theorem and states:

(length of hypotenuse)^2 = (length of one leg)^2 +
$\qquad\qquad\qquad\qquad$ (length of other leg)^2

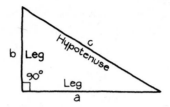

If we substitute the letters a, b, and c (as in the figure), the theorem can be more simply stated as:

$$c^2 = a^2 + b^2$$

The Pythagorean theorem can be used to find the length of one side when the other two sides are known. For example, if a = 8 cm and b = 6 cm, then $c = \sqrt{8^2 + 6^2}$; c = 10 cm.

$$c = \sqrt{a^2 + b^2}$$

$$a = \sqrt{c^2 - b^2}$$

$$b = \sqrt{c^2 - a^2}$$

RIGHT TRIANGLE EXERCISES

The right triangle formulas require calculation of square roots. They are easily done on a calculator with a square root key, but if your calculator does not have one, you should approximate the square roots to one decimal place accuracy. The following exercises will help you learn more about right triangles.

Use the guess and check method on your calculator to find $\sqrt{3}$. You know

$$\sqrt{1} < \sqrt{3} < \sqrt{4}$$

so you know $\sqrt{3}$ is between 1 and 2. Try:

$(1.5)^2 = 2.25$ too low
$(1.7)^2 = 2.89$ too low
$(1.8)^2 = 3.24$ too high

Since 2.89 is closest to 3, we pick 1.7 as the answer.

1. Use guess and check to calculate these to one decimal place accuracy.

 a. $\sqrt{5}$ b. $\sqrt{17}$ c. $\sqrt{64}$ d. $\sqrt{42.8}$

2. If a, b, and c represent the lengths of the sides of a right triangle, find the missing values.

    a. a = 9 cm   b = 12 cm   c =
    b. a = 17 m   b = 29 m   c =
    c. a =   b = 12 km   c = 13 km
    d. a =   b = 8 cm   c = 32 cm
    e. a = 15 m   b =   c = 29 m

3. Find two different right triangles having a perimeter of 15 cm.
For each, give the lengths of all three sides to two decimal
place accuracy. Hint: Use the guess and check method.

4. The hour hand of a small clock measures 3 cm while the
minute hand is 4 cm. What is the distance between the tips
of the hands at 3 o'clock?

5. A baseball diamond measures 90 feet between first and
second base. What is the distance from home plate to second
base?

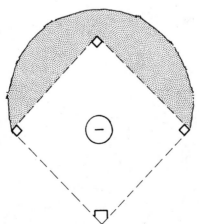

6. A 20 foot ladder is set against a building. If the base is five feet from the building, how high will the ladder reach? If it is moved in one foot, how much higher will it go?

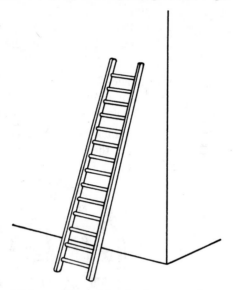

7. You are hiking with a friend when you come to point P. Your friend decides to walk to Q and then to R. You walk directly to R, and then wait for your friend. If you both walk at the rate of 4 km per hour, how long will you have to wait? Assume that PQR is a right triangle, with PQ being 8 km and QR being 6 km.

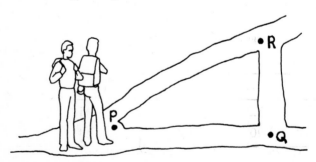

8. A hot air balloon is released in a wind that is blowing 24 km per hour. Without wind, the balloon would rise vertically at 4.3 km per hour. Find the total distance that the balloon

travels in one hour. Hint: The balloon travels along the diagonal of a right triangle.

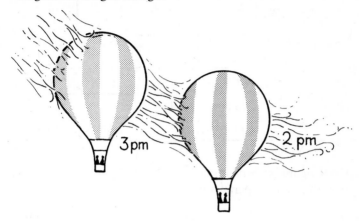

RIGHT TRIANGLE AREAS

Two identical right triangles can be put together to make a rectangle. From this picture one can see that the area of a right triangle is given by A = ½ab. Explain why.

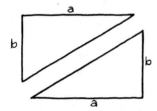 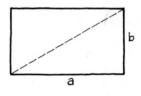

1. Find areas of right triangles with these legs.

a	b	area	a	b	area
2.5 km	7.2 km		82 in	80 in	
60 cm	90 cm		150 ft	250 ft	

2. The area formula for a right triangle can be rewritten to give a formula for a or a formula for b. Find these formulas, then find the missing values.

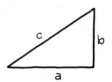

a	b	area	a	b	area
10 cm		100 cm²	456 cm		14592 cm²
	72.8 m	345 m²		123.4 m	6910.4 m²

3. This figure is made from two identical right triangles. Find the area and the perimeter of the figure if:

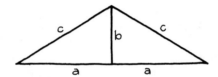

   a. a = 25 cm and b = 10 cm b. a = 15 cm and c = 20 cm

4. Write a formula for the area of the figure of exercise 3 in terms of a and b.

IRRATIONAL NUMBERS

Mathematics uses different symbols and names for numbers. We say, " two and six tenths" and write 2.6; or "one-third" and write ⅓ ; or "the square root of two" and write $\sqrt{2}$.

How big is $\sqrt{2}$? A right triangle helps give a picture of its size compared to other numbers. To use $\sqrt{2}$ in a calculation, you need to find its decimal value.

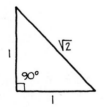

$$c^2 = 1^2 + 1^2$$
$$c^2 = 2$$
$$c = \sqrt{2}$$

By guess and check:

$$\sqrt{1} < \sqrt{2} < \sqrt{4}$$

1.4

By extraction, using paper and pencil:

$$
\begin{array}{r}
1.414 \\
\sqrt{2.0000} \\
2^{\underline{4}} \quad 1 \\
\hline
100 \\
96 \\
\hline
28^{\underline{1}} \quad 400 \\
281 \\
\hline
119^{00}
\end{array}
$$

By square root key on a calculator:

$$2 \ \sqrt{} \ = 1.4142135$$

By formulas and computers:

$$\sqrt{2} = 1.41421\ 35623\ 73095\ 04880\ 16887$$

It is known that $\sqrt{2}$ has a non-ending (infinite) but non-repeating (no pattern) decimal value. It is called an irrational number. Pick out the other irrational numbers in this group.

$$\sqrt{1} \quad \sqrt{2} \quad \sqrt{3} \quad \sqrt{4} \quad \sqrt{5} \quad \sqrt{6} \quad \sqrt{7} \quad \sqrt{8}$$
$$\downarrow \qquad\qquad\qquad \downarrow$$
$$1 \qquad\qquad\qquad 2$$

$$\sqrt{9} \quad \sqrt{10} \quad \sqrt{11} \quad \sqrt{12} \quad \sqrt{13} \quad \sqrt{14} \quad \sqrt{15} \quad \sqrt{16}$$

Another irrational number is called "pi" (pronounced pie) and is represented by the Greek letter π. It is the ratio of the circumference to the diameter of a circle. For every circle, the formula $\pi = C/d$ holds.

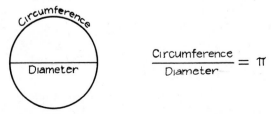

If you approximate π to 25 decimal places, you get this number:

$$\pi = 3.14159 \ \ 26535 \ \ 89793 \ \ 23846 \ \ 16433 \ \ \ldots$$

USING Π

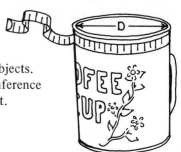

Carry out an experiment:
Get three different circular objects.
For each, measure the circumference and diameter. Fill in the chart.

Circumference	Diameter	$C \div d$

Average the three ratios; compare to 3.14.

The number π is used in many different formulas. Can you see how the circumference formula is developed from the formula $\pi = C/d$?

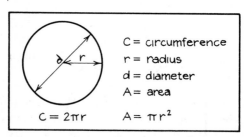

C = circumference
r = radius
d = diameter
A = area

$C = 2\pi r$ $A = \pi r^2$

If your calculator has a π key, you push that to get its decimal value. If there is no π key, learn an approximate value for π (3.14) and use it instead. Another very good approximation for π can be formed by dividing 355/113. Try it. This formula is easy to remember because it is formed by using pairs of the first three odd numbers (113355).

1. Find the circumference and area of the following circles.

a. Radius   5 cm   c. Diameter   30 cm

b. Radius   1 km   d. Diameter   15 m

2. A car tire has a radius of 33 cm. How far will it go in 1 revolution? How many revolutions will it take to go 1 km? Suppose the tire is inflated to a higher pressure and its radius increases to 34 cm. Now how many revolutions will it make per km?

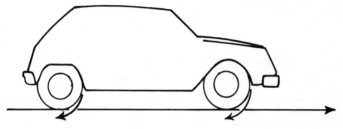

3. A coffee can has an outside circumference of 354 mm and a wall thickness of 1 mm. What is the inside diameter of the can?

4. A circle of greatest area is cut out of a 4 cm square of material. A square of greatest area is then cut out of the circle. How much material is wasted? Hint: Overlap the two figures in the right way. Or notice the dashed lines are legs of a right triangle.

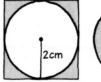

5. What is the area of the largest triangle that can be inscribed in a semi-circle of radius 6 cm?

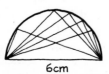

6cm

6. A square with sides 20 cm long is to be cut into circles in one of the ways pictured.

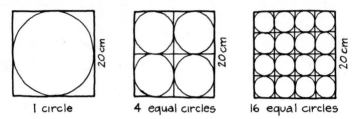

I circle   4 equal circles   16 equal circles

An 8-digit calculator with a π key gives an area of 314.15927 cm^2 for the large circle. Keying in 3.14 for π will result in 314 cm^2. Use either value to complete the chart.

Circles	Total area of circles	Total circumference of circles
1 large	314.15927 cm^2 or 314 cm^2	
4 medium		
16 small		

7. A company makes thin colored circular disks that are painted yellow on both sides. The disks are 4 cm in diameter, and each side receives two coats of paint. If a liter of paint will coat 12 square meters, how many disks will it paint?

VOLUME FORMULAS

Some area formulas extend easily to volume formulas.

$A = \ell \times w$ $\qquad\qquad\qquad$ $A = \pi r^2$

$\quad\downarrow$ $\qquad\qquad\qquad\qquad\quad$ $\downarrow$

$V = \ell \times w \times h$ $\qquad\qquad\quad$ $V = \pi r^2 h$

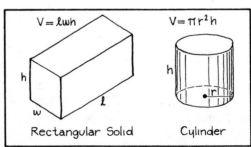

Rectangular Solid $\qquad\qquad$ Cylinder

1. A cereal box has a length of 19 cm, a width of 5 cm, and a height of 26 cm. What is its volume?

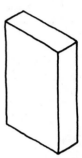

2. The above cereal box is filled to a height of 22 cm, and its contents weigh 369 gm. What is the density of the cereal in grams per cubic centimeter?

3. A large coffee can has an inside diameter of 18 cm and is filled to a height of 14 cm. What is the volume of its contents?

4. Write a formula for the volume of a cube using e as the length of an edge. Suppose the edge measures 7.5 cm. What is its volume? Suppose the cube has a volume of 640 cm^3. Find the length of an edge to the nearest .1 cm.

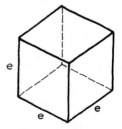

5. A cubical box has inside dimensions of 10 cm on each edge, and holds exactly 1 liter of water. How many cubic centimeters are there in a liter? At 4°C a liter of water has a mass of 1 kg. What is the mass of 1 cm^3 of water at this temperature?

6. Water weighs about one gram per cubic centimeter. A large bucket is in the shape of a right circular cylinder, with a diameter of 38 cm and a height of 52 cm. The empty bucket weighs 3 kg. What will it weigh when filled with water to a height of 50 cm?

7. How can you find the volume of this swimming pool? We have no special formula for it.

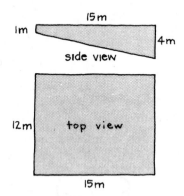

To solve it, divide the pool up into parts and make use of formulas you already know.

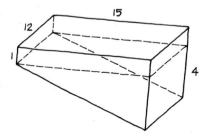

The top meter of the pool is a rectangular solid with dimensions 15 × 12 × 1 meters. What is it volume?

The bottom part is one half of a rectangular solid with what dimensions?

$$V = \frac{1}{2} \ell wh$$

What is its volume? What is the total volume of the pool? The owner decides to fill the pool using two garden hoses, each delivering 2000 liters per hour. How long will this take?

8. A ball has a diameter of 30 cm. Find its volume using the formula given.

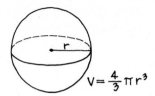

$V = \frac{4}{3} \pi r^3$

9. A rectangular chunk of wax has dimensions of 50 × 25 × 20 cm. It weighs 20 kg and costs $7.50.

   a. The wax is made into cylindrical candles as pictured. What will one candle weigh?

   b. What is the cost of the wax used in that candle?

10 cm

PROCEDURES

$$A = \ell \times w$$
$$V = \pi r^2 h$$

WHAT ARE THEY?

A formula is one way to express a plan (a procedure) for solving a problem. In this chapter we learn more information about procedures and ways to represent them.

The idea of a procedure is one of the most important ideas in problem solving. Computer scientists (people who study calculators and computers) have given a very precise definition.

A *procedure* is a step by step set of directions that can be mechanically interpreted and carried out by some agent. It is designed to try to solve a particular type of problem, but there is no guarantee of success.

There are four parts to the definition:

1. A Procedure is a set of directions.

2. The directions can be mechanically interpreted. Little or no thinking is required. Even a machine could do it.

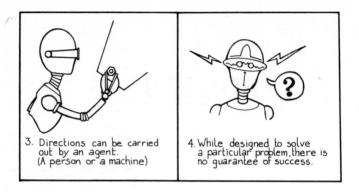

3. Directions can be carried out by an agent. (A person or a machine)

4. While designed to solve a particular problem, there is no guarantee of success.

WRITING PROCEDURES

1. A friend has a new calculator with a square root key. He wants to calculate $\sqrt{389.74}$. What directions would you give him or her to get the answer? Identify the agent.

2. Write down a procedure to be used to test if a calculator is functioning properly. Identify the agent. Will the procedure detect all possible malfunctions?

3. Write down a procedure for keeping score in:

   a. soccer   b. baseball   c. table tennis (ping-pong)

4. Write down a procedure for looking up a word that you know how to spell in the dictionary. The procedures should be general enough so it will work for every possible word. (What does your procedure do if the word is not in the dictionary?)

5. What is larger, $\frac{7}{13}$ or .54? Write down a procedure that uses a calculator to solve it. Then use your procedure to find the larger in these sets of numbers.

   a. $\frac{3}{8}$ .37   b. $\frac{9}{16}$ .55   c. $\frac{1}{11}$ .10

6. Simplify (reduce) each of the fractions as much as possible.

   $\frac{16}{18}$ $\frac{16}{80}$ $\frac{288}{1728}$

   Write down a procedure for reducing fractions.

IT'S NOT MATH

A procedure is a detailed step by step set of directions for solving a certain type of problem. Solving a math problem involves a mathematical procedure, with mathematical notation and vocabulary, but there are many problems that are not mathematics. A food recipe is a procedure designed to be carried out by a person with kitchen utensils. What problem is a recipe designed to solve? What is the meaning of each of the abbreviations used in the recipe?

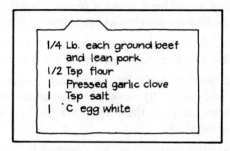

1/4 Lb. each ground beef
    and lean pork
1/2 Tsp flour
1   Pressed garlic clove
1   Tsp salt
1   C egg white

Piano music is a procedure for producing songs. The agent is usually a person aided by a piano. Notice the special notation and vocabulary. It takes many years of training and experience

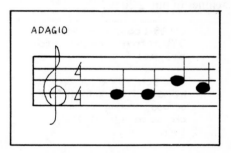

ADAGIO

for a person to become skilled at carrying out piano music procedures. But someone could produce piano music with the aid of other machines. It is very easy to use a player piano, a

record player or a tape player. They each follow a detailed step by step set of directions and help a person to solve a particular problem.

PROCEDURE PROBLEMS

1. Does owning a cookbook make a person a good cook? Why, or why not? Why do cookbooks use abbreviations?

2. Must a procedure be written in a form that is readable by a human? Give examples to support your answer.

3. Three common methods for calculating a square root are a) pencil and paper, b) math table, c) calculator with $\sqrt{\ }$ key. Compare/contrast these methods for ease of learning and for ease of using.

4. These crocheting instructions are designed to be carried out by a human. Make a list of the abbreviations in it. What does each mean? There exist machines that can knit or crochet automatically. What are some of the advantages/disadvantages of such machines in our society?

> CH 99 Loosely. Row 1: In
> 5th CH from hook, work (dc,
> ch 3, dc), *
>
> * SK 3 ch, Work (dc, ch3, dc)
> In next ch; Rep from *
> across, ending sk next
> ch, dc in last ch; ch 1,
> turn

5. A computer program is a procedure designed to be carried out by a computer. This sample program is written in BASIC, a language that can be "read" by both humans and computers. Read the program. A REM is a remark to help a human reader in following the steps of a program. What output will it produce? What problem does it solve?

```
10  Rem get lengths of sides
20  Let L = 25
30  Let W = 13
40  Rem compute area
50  Let A = L * W
60  Rem compute perimeter
70  Let P = 2 * L + 2 * W
80  Rem output answers
```

```
90 Print A,P
100 End
```

6. Give several more examples of procedures designed to be carried out by a combination of people and machines. In each case, identify the agent and the problem.

SAY IT IN ENGLISH

English and other spoken languages are called natural languages. One can use a natural language to write down a procedure. Writing down these steps in a careful and systematic way results in a *natural language procedure*. Compare the natural language procedure in the box to the formula $A = \ell w$. Which is easier to understand?

> To find the area of a rectangle:
> 1. Measure its length. Call this ℓ.
> 2. Measure its width. Call this w.
> 3. Multiply ℓ by w. The result is the area.

A palindromic number is a number that reads the same from left to right or right to left (i.e., 13731 or 512215). Here is a procedure that always leads to a palindromic number.

1. Pick any 2-digit number.   Examples:
2. Reverse the digits.   24   68
3. Add the two numbers.   + 42   + 86
4. Is it palindromic? If yes, stop. 66   154
5. If not, repeat steps two and   +451
   three. Try several more.   Finish this one

The number 6174 is a four-digit Jordanian number. It is the "answer" produced by the following procedure.

1. Select any four-digit number with at least two different digits.   7083
2. Arrange the digits from largest to smallest to make a number, and from smallest to largest to make a number.

    8730
   −0378
    8352

3. Subtract the smaller number from the larger.

    8352
   −2358
    6174

4. If the answer is 6174, stop. Other-
   wise, use the number starting   7641
   in step 2.   −1467
                                                    ‾‾‾‾‾‾
                                                     6174

Test the procedure for several different numbers. There is a three-digit Jordanian number. Find it.

A GRADING PROCEDURE

A major part of problem solving is figuring out solution procedures and writing them down. Writing a natural language procedure can be helpful, though it does take practice. Study the following example.

Mr. Teacher gives five tests during the term. A student's course grade is based upon the average of his best four scores, rounded to one decimal place.

Average	Course Grade
92.0 − 100	A
84.0 − 91.9	B
74.0 − 83.9	C
68.0 − 73.9	D
0 − 67.9	F

Give a natural language procedure for finding a student's test average and course grade.

A good way to begin is to make up some sample test scores and to process them. Think very carefully about the steps you follow. Try it for the set of scores: 69, 85, 63, 82, 84. Write down your procedure and compare it with the following.

1. Look at the scores of a student whose scores are to be processed.
2. Find the lowest of the student's five scores (and mentally eliminate it).
3. Add up the other four scores and divide the result by four. Record this as the student's average score.
4. Look in the table to find the student's letter grade. Record it.
5. Have all students in the class been processed? If 'no', go to step 1. If 'yes', stop.

YOU TRY IT

1. Use the natural language procedure and a calculator to complete the grade table.

Name	Test Scores 1	2	3	4	5	Test Average	Letter Grade
Adams	69	85	63	82	84		
Barns	95	0	98	92	100		
Davis	63	47	52	73	59		
Franklin	73	95	47	82	98		
Jones	89	78	94	82	82		

2. The students in Mr. Teachers class convince him that they should be allowed to throw out their two lowest scores. They want a grade based on the average of their best *three* scores. Write down a natural language procedure for determining a student's average and letter grade. Then determine the average score and letter grade for each student in Exercise 1.

3. A grocery store carries several different brands of each item. The brands usually come in different sizes of containers. Write down a natural language procedure for determining the "best buy" (that is, the cheapest per unit of measure). Then use a calculator and your procedure to find the best buy for each of the following items.

Item	Brand A	Brand B	Brand C	Brand D
Bread	$.76 for 1 lb.	$.95 for 18 oz.	$.45 for 12 oz.	$.56 for 14 oz.
Crackers	$.49 for 200 gm.	$1.98 for 1 kg.	—————	$.95 for 500 gm.
Juice	$1.25 per liter	————	$4.15 for 4 liters	$.79 for 250 ml.

4. How does one number lead to the next in this sequence?

$$14 \rightarrow 17 \rightarrow 50 \rightarrow 25 \rightarrow 29 \rightarrow 85 \rightarrow 89 \rightarrow$$

Hint: Think *squares*! Express the rule as a natural language procedure. Use it to find more terms of the above sequence, stopping when the sequence begins to cycle.

5. Workers are paid their regular hourly rate of pay for the first 40 hours worked in a week. A worker is paid "time-and-a-half" (that is, 1½ times the regular rate) for the hours worked beyond 40. Give a natural language procedure for calculating

each worker's pay and the total payroll for a company. Then use your procedure to process the following data.

Name	Hours Worked	Pay Rate	Total Pay
Adams	40	$4.36	
Jones	34	$5.72	
Morris	46	$3.87	
Smith	54.5	$8.42	
Taylor	38	$4.95	

Total payroll

6. The workers in this company negotiate a new contract which sets the above rates of pay for the first 32 hours. They receive time-and-a-half for the hours after that, up to 40 hours. They receive double pay for all hours above 40. Write a natural language procedure for calculating each worker's pay and the total payroll. Use it to process the data given above.

7. See if you can figure out a procedure for getting the 20th number in this sequence.

$$1, 1, 2, 3, 5, 8, 13, 21, \ldots$$

Write down a natural language procedure for finding more terms and try working it yourself. Then trade papers with someone and work through each other's! Compare your statements and decide which is the easier to follow.

FLOWCHARTS

Computer scientists often use *flowcharts* to represent procedures. A flowchart is a set of directions in boxes, connected by arrows. To make flowcharts easier to read, people have decided to assign meanings to the special shapes.

For example the beginning and end(s) of a flowchart are indicated by elliptical boxes.

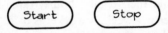

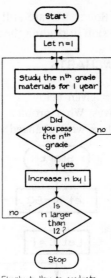

Flowchart: How to graduate
from high school

An action that is to be carried out is indicated in a rectangular box.

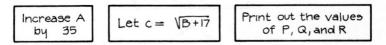

A diamond box is used for decision making. In it a yes-no question is asked.

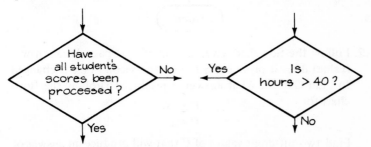

At one time computer scientists thought that flowcharts were very useful in figuring out how to solve a problem. Now they have decided that natural language procedures are a better tool. Flowcharts are good for displaying certain procedures in a textbook or on the blackboard. There they give a picture of the overall process. Thus flowcharts are still widely used and it is worthwhile to develop skill in reading them.

FOLLOW THE FLOWCHARTS

1. Follow the flowchart given below. Explain in simple English what problem it solves. What problem would be solved if the "Increase C by 1" box were changed to "Increase C by 2"?

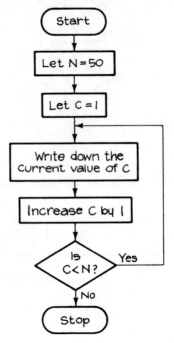

2. Follow the flowchart given at top of next page. What answer (value) does it produce? Suppose the second box is changed to "Let C = 3". What answer is produced? Follow the flowchart for

$$C = 16$$
$$C = 15$$

Find two different values of C that will produce an answer of 10.

3. Have you had trouble following any of the flowcharts? It is sometimes helpful to make a table showing the variables and their changing values. Here is one way you could set up a

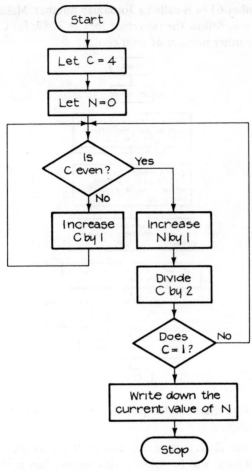

table to help you with flowchart # 2. Make a table for C = 12, then for any number of your choice.

C	N	Remarks
4		Let C = 4
4	0	Let N = 0
4	1	If C even, increase N by 1
2	1	Divide C by 2
2	2	C ≠ 1 so N increased by 1
1	2	Divide C by 2

4. The number 6174 is called a Jordanian number. Make a table
   to help you follow the flowchart for C = 3087; for C = 1874;
   for some other number of your choice.

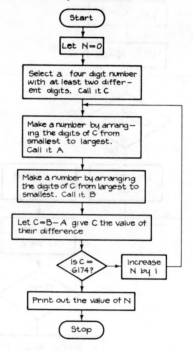

5. Draw a flowchart for the palindromic procedure given earlier
   in this chapter.

6. Follow the flowchart at the top of the next page. Explain
   what problem will be solved if the second box is changed so
   that the initial value of B is 7.

7. Carry out the procedure given in the flowchart at the bottom
   of the next page for each of these values.

   a. V = 27
   b. V = −13
   c. V = −94
   d. V = 16

   What problem does this procedure solve?

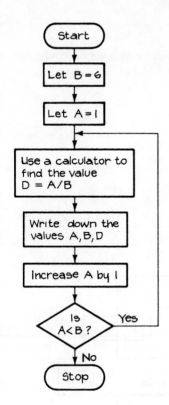

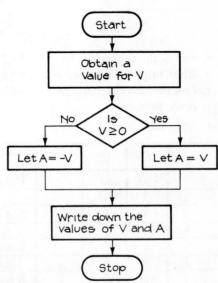

PRACTICE WITH A TABLE

Tables are particularly useful in following a very complicated procedure. Study the completed table below along with the flowchart.

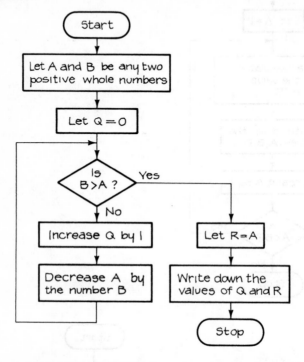

a. Finish the tables for the cases A=7, B=2, and A=12, B=4.
b. What problem is solved by the procedure in the flowchart?
c. Follow the flowchart (with or without a table) for the case A=5, B=0.

Explain the results.

A	B	Q	R	Remarks
7	3	—	—	Values given
7	3	0	—	
7	3	1	—	B is not greater than A
4	3	1	—	A decreased
4	3	2	—	B not greater than A
1	3	2	—	A is decreased
1	3	2	1	B is greater than A

A	B	Q	R
7	2		

A	B	Q	R
12	4		

Output from flowchart is Q = 2, R = 1.

NEWTON'S METHOD

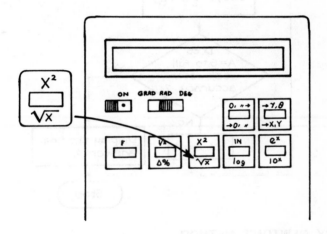

Many calculators have a square root key. To calculate $\sqrt{17}$, you push the keys

1	7	$\sqrt{}$

After a brief pause, the result 4.1231056 is displayed. When this number is squared on an 8-digit calculator the result is 16.999999, which means we have a close approximation to $\sqrt{17}$.

The calculator uses Newton's method to calculate square roots. This method is named after Isaac Newton (1642 – 1727), a famous English mathematician and scientist. The flowchart for Newton's method is shown on the next page. Any positive initial guess, such as G = 1, will work. The procedure is well suited to a calculator's capabilities.

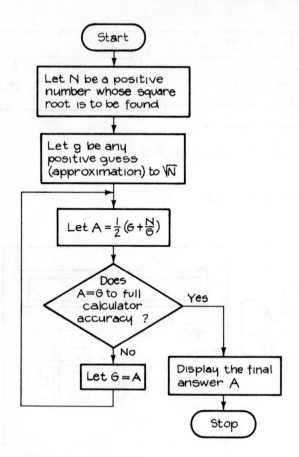

TRY NEWTON'S METHOD

Let's study an example, to see how Newton's method works. We will look at N = 17 and use an intial guess G = 4. Observe that $4 < \sqrt{17}$, and $\sqrt{17} < 17/4$. That is, the two numbers 4

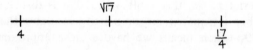

and 17/4 bracket $\sqrt{17}$. The Newton process uses a point midway between these two as the next guess. The averaging

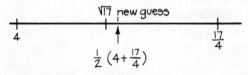

process is used over and over again. The two numbers G and N/G will always bracket $\sqrt{N}$. Mathematicians have proved that in this averaging process the bracketing numbers will get closer and closer together.

1. Complete the following table.

N	G	N/G	$A = \frac{1}{2}(G + N/G)$	Remarks
17	4			Initial values.
17	4	4.25	4.125	Calculate N/G and average.
17	4.125			
17				

2. Follow the flowchart for N = 17 and G = 1. Write down each value of A. Stop when A and G differ by less than .000001 in the decision box step.

3. Follow the Newton method flowchart for N=144 and G=12. Explain what happens.

4. Newton also developed a method for calculating cube roots and higher roots. Replace the "Let A = $\frac{1}{2}$ (G + N/G)" by "Let A = $\frac{1}{3}$ [2G + (N/G^2)]" in the square root flowchart. It will now calculate cube roots. Try it using N=8 and G=1, recording the results in a table. Stop when A and G differ by less than .0001 in the decision box step.

5. Newton's method for calculating fourth roots uses the formula:

$$A = \frac{1}{4}[3G + (N/G^3)]$$

Use it to calculate a fourth root of 16 using an initial guess of 1. Record the results in a table, stopping when A and G differ by less than .0001.

6. Notice the pattern of these formulas. Extend the pattern to

Square root	$A = \frac{1}{2}\left(G + \frac{N}{G}\right)$
Cube root	$A = \frac{1}{3}\left(2G + \frac{N}{G^2}\right)$
Fourth root	$A = \frac{1}{4}\left(3G + \frac{N}{G^3}\right)$

make a formula for calculating fifth roots. Try it on the
problem N=32 using an initial guess of G=1. Record the
results in a table, stopping when A and G differ by less than
.0001.

CALCULATOR MEMORY

STORAGE SPACE

Every calculator has a memory. The word *memory* just means storage space where numbers and operations can be stored.

Picture a calculator's memory as mail boxes whose contents can change. A calculator "memory box" is like a variable. It has a name and it can contain a value which you can change.

What happens as you key the calculation 12 + 58 = into a calculator? You push the 1 key; the number 1. is stored in a calculator memory box and also is displayed in the video display. You push the 2 box; now 12 is stored and displayed. You push the + key. The calculator stores (remembers) which operation key you have pushed. You continue by keying in the 58. The calculator stores and displays this value. Finally you push the = key. This directs the calculator to carry out the (stored) operation + on the pair of (stored) numbers 12 and 58.

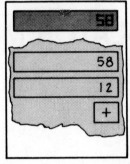

Some calculators have a larger memory than others, which means they can store more numbers and operations. This is useful in more complicated calculations such as

$$(89.37 \times 62.3) \quad + \quad (.492 \times 6.71)$$

         Part 1   Part 2

It is easy to do the Part 1 or the Part 2 calculation, but additional memory is needed to store the answer to Part 1 while the calculator is carrying out the calculation of Part 2. After the answer to Part 2 is computed it is added to the (stored) answer to Part 1.

MEMORY MACHINES

1. An automatic elevator has a memory. It can remember which floor number buttons have been pushed. It has circuitry to stop at those floors in a logical order. Give several examples of other machines or devices that have a memory. Which of the examples you chose has the largest memory (that is, can store the most information)?

2. A number that has just been keyed into a calculator can be erased (set to 0.) by pushing the CE (clear entry) key. This allows one to correct an error. Consider the machines listed in examples above. Which of them have a "CE" facility so that an error can be corrected?

3. Most calculators lose their memory contents when turned off. That is, when the calculator is turned back on, the memory contents have been erased. Does your calculator do this? A checkbook calculator is designed to fit into a checkbook holder in one's purse or pocket. It stores a bank balance, even

when turned off. Write down several other calculator applications where such "permanent" memory would be useful.

4. A computer has a memory like a calculator, but generally much larger. Write down a problem where a very large memory is needed for its solution.

5. On some calculators if you key the sequence 5 + 9 × 8 = you will get the mathematically correct answer of 77. Explain why such a calculator must have at least three memory locations for storing numbers and two memory locations for storing operations.

SIMPLE MEMORY

Let's look at the memory system on a simple 4-function video display calculator. It has storage space for three numbers and an operation. We will name them (label them) as follows. S_1 is read "S sub one".

S_1 [＿＿＿＿＿＿＿]   Op [＿＿＿＿＿＿＿]
S_2 [＿＿＿＿＿＿＿]   Op is short for "Operation"
A [＿＿＿＿＿＿＿] $(+, -, \times, \div)$

Follow what happens in these memory locations as the calculation 45 × 73 = is keyed. We begin with the calculator just turned on and/or cleared.

S_1 [0.   ]   Op [none   ]
S_2 [0.   ]
A [0.   ]   Memory is clear.

Key in the number 45. It is stored in S_1 and displayed.

S_1 [45.   ]   Op [none   ]
S_2 [0.   ]   45 has been keyed
A [0.   ]   and is displayed.

Next you depress the × operation key. On almost all calculators this causes two things to happen. The × is stored in the Op location and a copy of the contents of S_1 is made and placed in S_2.

S_1 [45.   ]   Op [×   ]
S_2 [45.   ]   45 × has been keyed.
A [0.   ]

Next key in the number 73. It replaced the 45. in S_1 and is displayed.

S_1	73.	Op	X
S_2	45.		45 X 73 has been keyed.
A	0.		

Finally, push the = key. This tells the calculator to carry out the operation stored in Op on the numbers stored in S_1 and S_2. The *arithmetic register*, storage location A, is used for this. The answer is placed in A. Then a copy is made and placed in S_1.

S_1	3285.	Op	X
S_2	45.		The calculation has
A	3285.		been completed.

Notice that when the calculation is finished each memory location has something in it. What do you think would happen if the = key were pushed again. Test out your guess on a calculator.

1. Show the memory contents for each step in the calculation 9 X 4.

S_1	0.	Op	none
S_2	0.		Memory is
A	0.		clear.

S_1		Op	
S_2			9 keyed
A			in.

S_1		Op	
S_2			9 X is
A			keyed in.

S_1		Op	
S_2			9 X 4 is
A			keyed in.

S_1		Op	
S_2			9 X 4 = is
A			keyed in.

AUTOMATIC CONSTANT

Suppose the calculation $3 \times 5 =$ has just been completed. The memory contents will be:

S_1 [15.]   Op [$\times$]
S_2 [3.]
A   [15.]

On most calculators, pushing the = key (again) will cause the operation in Op to be carried out on the contents of S_1 and S_2. Try this on your calculator. If the result of $3 \times 5 = =$ is 45, then your calculator has an *automatic constant for multiplication*.

1. Use this feature to calculate:

   a. $3^2 \times 5$ b. $3^3 \times 5$ c. $3^8 \times 5$ d. $9^5 \times 845$

   Hint: Compare the answers from $3 \times 5 = =$ and $5 \times 3 = =$. What number stays in S_1 and acts as the constant multiplier in each case?

2. Most calculators will display the answer of 36 for the keying sequence 6 $\times$ = . Does your calculator square a number in this manner? Explain how/why this works in terms of calculator memory. Then use this automatic squaring feature as you calculate $\sqrt{30}$ to the nearest tenth by the guess and check method.

3. Most calculators have an automatic constant for division. Key in $16 \div 2 = =$. The result on a calculator with automatic constant for division will be 4. Explain why, using memory boxes. Then carry out the following calculations.

   a. $16 \div 2 \div 2 \div 2$ b. $72.6 \div 6.9 \div 6.9 \div 6.9 \div 6.9$

   c. $1728 \div 3 \div 3 \div 3$ d. $1024 \div 2^{10}$

4. Suppose you are using a calculator that has an automatic constant for division. You key in the sequence 5 $\div$ = = . Determine the result *without* using a calculator. Check by using a calculator. Explain.

   Some calculators have a 1/x key. This key calculates the reciprocal of a number. To calculate 1/5 one keys [5] [1/x] . The answer is displayed, and is stored in S_1. Find the reciprocals of the following numbers.

   5   83   62   −8   .5   .25

5. What do you expect the result to be when you key 3 + = into your calculator? Try it. Did it come out as you expected? Most calculators will give 3 as the answer because they *do not* have an automatic constant for addition or subtraction. For such a calculator, the sequence C 3 + *does not* put a copy of S_1 into S_2. This is different from the way the $\times$ and $\div$ keys work. Test your calculator to see if it has an automatic constant for subtraction and record the results.

6. Consider the sequence 5 + $\times$ 6 =. What do you think the result will be for your calculator? Try it. Explain how your calculator's memory system handles the sequence of operations + $\times$.

7. When the C key is pushed, the S_1, S_2, and A memory locations are set to 0. and the Op location is set to "none." Explain what the **CE** key does to the S_1 and Op locations on your calculator.

USING AUTOMATIC CONSTANTS

We have discussed the automatic constant for multiplication features that most calculators have. Two applications of this feature are illustrated in the following examples.

TEST
1. Key in 6 $\times$ =
2. If the result is 36, your calculator has an automatic constant for multiplication.

---

1. The formula for compound interest is $A = P(1+R)^T$.

   P = initial principal   T = number of time periods

   R = interest rate per time period

   A = final amount of money

   For example, suppose that $150 is deposited in a bank that pays 4% interest per year, compounded quarterly. How much money will there be after one year? In this problem P = 150, R = .01 (the interest for one quarter of a year is 1%) and T = 4 (one year is 4 quarters). Thus the calculation to be performed is $A = 150(1+.01)^4 = 150(1.01)^4$

   $$A = 150 \times 1.01 \times 1.01 \times 1.01 \times 1.01$$

This is ideally suited to a calculator with automatic constant for multiplication. We key in 1.01 × 150 = = = = and get the final answer $156.09 (rounded to the nearest cent).

a. Do the above calculation on your own calculator and record the unrounded result.
b. Find the final amount of money that results if $275 is deposited in a bank paying 4% per year, compounded quarterly, and left in for one year.
c. Solve (b) using an interest rate of 6% per year.
d. Solve (c) assuming that the bank compounds interest 12 times per year (interest rate per time period is 6/12 per cent.)
e. Solve (c) assuming that the bank compounds interest 24 times per year (interest rate is 6/24 per cent).

2. Percentage decrease and percentage markup problems are easily done using an automatic constant, even when a calculator does not have a % key. Suppose we have the price of several items and want to increase each by 36%.

Original price $6.50

$6.50 + 36% of $6.50
= 6.50 + .36 × 6.50
= 1.36 × 6.50
= 8.84

Original price $9.47

$9.47 + 36% of $9.47
= 9.47 + .36 × 9.47
= 1.36 × 9.47
= 12.88 (rounded)

That is, increasing the price by 36% is exactly the same as multiplying by 1.36.

Examine your calculator display as you key in 1.36 × 6.5 = 9.47 =. After the first = the answer 8.84 is displayed. After the second =, 12.8792 is displayed. Use a memory diagram to explain how/why keying this sequence solved both percent-age problems. Then solve the following problems.

a. Increase each of the following by 28%.

      $8.90 $6.45 $12.87 $47.13

b. Decrease each of the following by 34%. Hint: $1 - .34 = .66$.

      $6.50 $4.90 $16.75 $75.

c. The price of an item was increased by 35%. The final price is given below. Find the original price. Use guess and check, showing all of your work.

      $32.40 $85.

MIXED CHAIN CALCULATIONS

Carry out the following calculation on your calculator.

$$(82.4 \times 79.6) - (65.9 \times 38.4) + (1897.6 \div 1.87)$$

One can view this as a chain of different types of calculations. It consists of three distinct multiplications/divisions whose results are to be combined by subtraction and addition. We can do the problem with a calculator, using pencil and paper to record the results of the multiplications/divisions. After completing the three multiplications/divisions, we can use a calculator to complete the calculation.

$$
\begin{aligned}
82.4 \times 79.6 &= 6559.04 \\
-65.9 \times 38.4 &= -2530.56 \\
1897.6 \div 1.87 &= \underline{1014.7593} \\
\text{ANSWER} &= 5043.2393
\end{aligned}
$$

A little thought shows that one only needs to write down the results of the first two multiplications. The results from the division can be left in the calculator (it is in S_1) and can be combined with the +6550.04 and the −2530.56.

What role does pencil and paper play in doing the calculation? It serves as a temporary memory. The intermediate results +6559.04 and −2530.56 are stored on paper until they are needed. Writing them down and later keying them into the calculator takes considerable time and can lead to errors. A calculator with extra memory can overcome these two difficulties.

Many calculators have extra memory that is useful in mixed chain calculations. There are several good ways to design a calculator with extra memory. After studying two of the more common methods, you can compare and contrast the two. It may be that your calculator has extra memory different from each of these. If so, you will need to refer to your owner's manual for details. The general ideas about extra memory given here will help you to understand the owner's manual.

Solve the problems given below without using the "extra" memory features of your calculator. Show the details of your work. Give clear indication of where pencil and paper are used to store temporary (intermediate) results.

1. $\dfrac{87.6 \times 34.5 - 62.9 \times 13.8}{27.6}$

2. $\dfrac{3}{7} + \dfrac{8}{19} - \dfrac{2}{13}$

3. Let m be the mean of 79, 85, 62, 87, 93. Calculate:

$$\frac{(79-m)^2 + (85-m)^2 + (62-m)^2 + (87-m)^2 + (93-m)^2}{5}$$

To find m calculate
$$(79+85+62+87+93)/5$$

4. Use guess and check to calculate the square roots to one decimal place and find the sum $\sqrt{2} + \sqrt{3}$.

5. Fill in the missing values on the bill.

Sold to:

Terry Jones
47 East 87th Street

Item	Quantity	Each	Total
Hinges	25	$ .17	$4.25
Nails	18 Pounds	.37	
Paint	12 Gallons	5.72	
Thinner	3 Gallons	1.72	

Subtotal _____
+6% sales tax _____
Grand total _____

FOUR KEY MEMORY SYSTEM

Notice the four "M" keys in the calculator pictured. These four keys indicate the calculator has a four key memory system. This is the most common system found on inexpensive calculators. You should learn how it works even if your present calculator uses a different memory system.

The four extra keys are designed to interact with a single memory location, which we will call M. The memory location

M, like S_1, S_2, and A, can store a number.

CM
The CM (clear memory) key sets the memory location M to zero. We denote this by CM: $0. \to M$

RM
The other three keys involve both M and S_1. RM (recall memory) makes a copy of the contents of M and places it into S_1. We denote this by: RM: $M \to S_1$.
The contents of M remain unchanged in M.

M+
The M+ key adds S_1 to M and places the answer in M. M+: $M + S_1 \to M$
The contents of S_1 remain unchanged in S_1.

M−
The M− key subtracts S_1 from M and places the answer in M. M−: $M - S_1 \to M$
The contents of S_1 remain unchanged in S_1.

FOUR KEY MEMORY EXAMPLE

Use a calculator with four key memory and follow along as we solve the problem:

$$(9 \times 7) - (24 \div 6)$$

Step 1: Calculator is turned on   Step 2: 9×7 is keyed.

S_1 [0.] M [0.] S_1 [7.] M [0.]
S_2 [0.] Op [none] S_2 [9.] Op [×]
A [0.]   A [0.]

Step 3: = is keyed   Step 4: M+ is keyed.

S_1 [63.] M [0.] S_1 [63.] M [63.]
S_2 [9.]   Op [×] S_2 [9.]   Op [×]
A [63.]   A [63.]

Note: The quantity 9×7 has been calculated and placed in M.

Step 5: $24 \div 6$ is keyed.   Step 6: = is keyed.

S_1 [6.]   M [63.] S_1 [4.]   M [63.]
S_2 [24.] Op [÷] S_2 [24.] Op [÷]
A [63]   A [4.]

Note: We have just calculated $24 \div 6$ and are ready to subtract it from M.

Step 7: M− is keyed.   Step 8: RM is keyed.

S_1 [6.] M [59.] S_1 [59.] M [59.]

S_2 [24.] Op [−] S_2 [24.] Op [−]

A [59.]   A [59.] The final answer
                                                   59. is displayed.

MEMORY PROBLEMS

Each of the exercises which follow are designed to be done on a calculator with a four key memory system.

1. Work the example given on the previous page. Then repeat the calculations, but this time leave out steps 3 and 6. Most calculators will give the same result. Does yours? What does this experiment show about the M+ and M− keys?

2. Calculate:
$$87 \times 39 - 46 \times 58 + 6467 \div 29$$

3. Calculate:
$$\frac{1}{2} + \frac{1}{3} + \frac{1}{4} + \frac{1}{5}$$
Did you get 1.2833333?

4. Carry out the following calculations and at the same time find the sum of the answers.

    89.4 ÷ 17.2 + 16.3 =

    72.5 − 63.2 × 9.4 =

    397 + 285 ÷ 16.3 = _____

                Sum =

    Hint: M is not needed in doing the three separate calculations above.

5. Without using a calculator determine the contents of M after the following sequence of calculations. Check using your calculator.

    a. CM C   3 M+ M− 2   M− M+   RM

    b. CM C   12 M+ ×   =   M+

    c. CM C   10 M+ ×   =   M+ =   M+

6. Carry out the experiment:

$$\text{CM} \quad 1 \quad 0 \quad \text{M+} \quad 5 \quad \div \quad \text{RM} \quad =$$

The first four steps put 10 into M. The remaining steps show how a number in M can be used as a divisor for a number in S_1. The answer is $5 \div 10 = .5$. Use this idea to solve the following problems without writing down the intermediate results.

a. $\dfrac{5}{16 \div 40 + 1}$ b. $\dfrac{289.7 \times 16.4 - 76.8}{185.4 + 16.9 + 28.4}$

c. $\dfrac{6972 \div 13.8 + 276.3}{89.4 \times 17.6 - 3894 \div 16.4 + 14.7}$

d. Add the answers to a, b, and c. Do you get 24.412578?

7. Show the contents of each memory storage location after each step given below. Without using a calculator, determine the final answer that will be displayed. Check by using a calculator.

   a. CM C 5 M− × 6 = M+ RM

   b. CM C 8 M+ ÷ 2 = M− RM

   c. CM C 4.5 + 3.5 = M+ 7.5 − 2.5 = × RM

8. Mentally devise a plan for carrying out the following calculations on your calculator, and then carry out the calculations.

   a. $(192.87 - 68.943) \times (672.8 + 347.29)$

   b. $(945.82 - 671.87) \ (329.89 + 61.32)$

TWO KEY MEMORY SYSTEM

There are many ways to add one memory location to a simple calculator. The two key memory system pictured on the next page is fairly common. It has a single extra memory location M, just as does the four key memory system calculator. It will be used in a different way.

RM The RM key works just like RM on a four key system.
       RM: $M \rightarrow S_1$ (M is unchanged.)

M   The M key is used with each of the keys C, =, +, −, ×, and ÷. In each case S_1, S_2, and Op are not changed.

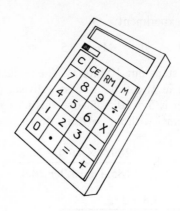

Keying Sequence		Results
M	C	Sets M to 0.
M	=	$S_1 \rightarrow M$
M	+	$M + S_1 \rightarrow M$ Just like M+ and
M	−	$M - S_1 \rightarrow M$ M− on the four key system.
M	X	$M \times S_1 \rightarrow M$
M	÷	$M \div S_1 \rightarrow M$

Suppose, for example, that one wants to carry out the following calculation.

$$87 \times 39 - 46 \times 58 + 6467 \div 29$$

The following key sequence can be used.

Step	Keying sequence	Results
1	M C	Set M to 0.
2	87 X 39 =	Calculates 87×39.
3	M +	Adds above results to M. Result is in M.
4	46 X 58 =	Calculates 46×58.
5	M −	Subtracts above result from M. Result is in M.
6	6467 − 29 =	Calculates $6467 - 29$.

| 7 | M + | Adds above result to M.
Result is in M. |
| 8 | RM | Displays final answer. |

1. If you have access to a calculator with a two key memory system, use it to solve the following problems.

 a. $\dfrac{1}{2} + \dfrac{1}{3} + \dfrac{1}{4} + \dfrac{1}{5}$

 b. $89.4 - 17.2 + 16.3 =$

 $725 - 63.2 \times 9.4 =$

 $397 + 285 - 16.3 =$ _____

 Sum =

2. Give some advantages of a four key memory system over a two key memory system. Give some advantages of a two key memory system over a four key memory system. Which seems best to you?

3. Suppose that a calculator has two "extra" memory locations named M and N. It has four keys labeled RM, RN, M, and N. The M and N locations work like on the two key memory system. Write down a sequence of steps to solve the following problem on the calculator.

$$\frac{87.3 \times 16.3 - 93.5 \div 2.8}{44.3 \div 3.8 + 69.4 \times 24.3}$$

FRACTIONS

Some fraction calculations are quite simple and can be done mentally. Do these examples mentally.

$\dfrac{1}{2} + \dfrac{1}{3} =$

$\dfrac{1}{2} - \dfrac{1}{3} =$

$2 \div (\dfrac{1}{3}) =$

$\dfrac{1}{12} + \dfrac{1}{4} =$

Simple fraction problems occur in a variety of real-world situations. For example, consider $2 \div (1/3)$. I have two pounds of hamburgers. A recipe calls for ⅓ of a pound per person. How many people will my two pounds serve? It is convenient to solve this problem mentally.

Sometimes you have a fraction calculation that is hard to do mentally or using pencil and paper. A calculator with memory easily handles a problem such as

$$\tfrac{3}{8} + \tfrac{5}{14} - \tfrac{2}{9}$$

Of course, when such a problem is done on a calculator, the result is usually a complicated decimal expression. This can be embarrassing if the answer can also be expressed as a simple fraction. The calculator answer for $\tfrac{1}{12} + \tfrac{1}{4}$ is .3333333, which we recognize as $\tfrac{1}{3}$. However, $\tfrac{1}{3} + \tfrac{1}{4}$ gives .5833333 on a calculator, and most people do not recognize this as $\tfrac{7}{12}$.

1. Solve mentally and then with a calculator.

   a. $\tfrac{1}{3} + \tfrac{1}{3}$ d. $\tfrac{5}{12} - \tfrac{1}{3}$ g. $\tfrac{3}{4} - \tfrac{5}{8}$

   b. $\tfrac{1}{2} + \tfrac{3}{8}$ e. $\tfrac{1}{3} + \tfrac{1}{6}$ h. $\tfrac{1}{2} - \tfrac{1}{6}$

   c. $\tfrac{3}{8} + \tfrac{5}{8}$ f. $\tfrac{3}{10} - \tfrac{1}{5}$ i. $\tfrac{1}{2} + \tfrac{1}{3} + \tfrac{1}{6}$

2. Given below are some calculator answers to fraction calculation problems. Find simple fractions whose calculator values are the same as these.

   a. .3333333   d. .6666666   g. .4444444

   b. .1666666   e. .1111111   h. .875

   c. .375   f. .625   i. .8333333

USE YOUR MEMORY

The problems given below involve substantial amounts of calculation. The memory features of a calculator may be helpful.

1. Suppose that a population is growing at the rate of 2% per year. The following formula can be used to predict the population in the future.

   $$A = P(1 + R)^T$$

   > P = initial population
   > R = growth rate per year
   > T = number of years
   > A = final population

Thus if the intial population is 240,000 and it grows 2% per year for five years, the final population will be $A = 240000 \times (1.02)^5$. Find this on your calculator. Notice that the population growth formula is exactly the same as the compound interest formula. How many years will it take for the population to double at this growth rate?

2. Suppose that a country has five provinces, whose initial populations and yearly growth rate are as follows.

Province	Initial Population	% Yearly Growth Rate
A	167,000	2.5
B	41,200	1.8
C	39,700	2.1
D	294,000	.3
E	43,900	1.2

Determine what the country's total population will be in five years if these growth rates continue for that period of time. What will it be in 10 years?

THE NUMBER e

Examine the sequence

$$(1 + \frac{1}{1})^1 = 2$$

$$(1 + \frac{1}{2})^2 = 2.25$$

$$(1 + \frac{1}{3})^3 = 2.37037$$

$$(1 + \frac{1}{n})^n \text{ for } n = 1, 2, \ldots$$

The terms of this sequence will get closer and closer together as n increases. They will converge to a number which mathematicians denote by the letter e. It is an irrational number.

$$e = 2.71828\ 18284\ 59045 \ldots$$

The number e is quite important in higher mathematics, such as in calculus. Thus come calculators have an e key. Some calculators have an ln key (natural logarithm key), which is a function involving the number e.

1. Calculate $(1 + \frac{1}{n})^n$ for n = 4, 5, . . . 10. How far is the last value from e?

2. The value of e is also given by

$$1 + (1/1!) + (1/2!) + (1/3!) + (1/4!) + \ldots + (1/n!) + \ldots$$

Recall that 1! = 1, 2! = 2 × 1 = 2, 3! = 3 × 2 × 1 = 6, etc. Calculate the sum up through the (1/10!) term. How much does this sum differ from e?

CALCULATOR ARITHMETIC

THE NUMBER LINE

By now you are aware that calculator arithmetic is not exactly the same as "real" arithmetic. The 8-digit accuracy is the main source of difference.

Every point on the real number line corresponds to a number, and vice versa.

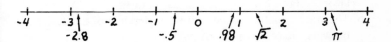

You know that the set of real numbers is infinite. There is no largest real number, no smallest real number and no non-zero real number that is closest to zero. There are an infinite number of points (i.e., numbers) on the number line. Between any two numbers, you can always find another one.

On a calculator number line:
1. There is a largest (positive) number.
2. There is a smallest (negative) number.
3. There are two non-zero numbers that are closest to zero.
4. There are holes or gaps.
5. There are only a finite number of points.

WARNING
Throughout this chapter we limit our attention to a simple 8-digit calculator that does not use scientific notation. But not even all simple 8-digit calculators use the same number line and/or arithmetic.

NUMBER LINE PROBLEMS

1. Start with 1.0 in your calculator display. Repeatedly divide it by 10 until an underflow occurs. (This happens when you unexpectedly get zero as an answer.) The result immediately before the underflow is the smallest positive number your calculator can display. What is it? What is the negative number closest to zero on your calculator?

2. Find the smallest 10 positive numbers on your calculator's number line. Write them down on this diagram in order, starting with the smallest.

What is the difference between each successive pair of numbers?

3. Use your calculator to display the numbers found in 2 above. Continue to explore your calculator's number line in the range of 0 to 1. Complete the following sentences.

   a. In the range 0 to 1 inclusive, the number line for my calculator contains exactly _____ points.
   b. They are equally spaced, with a difference of _____ between successive pairs of points.

4. Use your calculator to display the negative of each of the numbers in problem 2.
   Continue to explore the numbers you can locate from −1 to 0, and complete the following sentences.

   a. My calculator contains _____ points on its number line from −1 to 0 inclusive.
   b. Each successive pair of equally spaced numbers are _____ apart.

5. Use your calculator to find each of the following calculator numbers.

   a. The smallest number above 1. How much larger than 1. is it?
   b. The smallest number above 10. How much larger than 10. is it?
   c. The smallest number above 100. How much larger than 100 is it?

    d. The smallest number above 1000. How much larger than 1000 is it?

    e. The smallest number above 10000000. How much larger than 10000000 is it?

6. Complete the following sentences.

    a. In the range 1. to 10. inclusive, the number line for my calculator contains _____ points. They are equally spaced, with a difference of _____ between successive pairs of points.

    b. In the range 100. to 1000. inclusive, the number line for my calculator contains _____ points. They are equally spaced, with a difference of _____ between successive pairs of points.

    c. In the range 100000. to 1000000. inclusive, the number line for my calculator contains _____ points. They are equally spaced, with a difference of _____ between successive pairs of points.

    d. In the range −10000000. to −1000000. inclusive, the number line for my calculator contains _____ points.
(Hint: This is the same as for 1000000. to 10000000.)
They are equally spaced, with a difference of _____ between successive pairs of numbers.

    e. The largest number on my calculator's number line is _____ and the negative of this is _____, (which is the smallest number). The points on the number line are not equally spaced. The smallest difference between numbers is _____, which holds for numbers between _____ and _____. The largest spacing is _____, which holds for numbers between _____ and _____, and also for numbers between _____ and _____.

CALCULATOR ARITHMETIC

Calculator arithmetic is peculiar! Study the example, and do it on your calculator. You know that if A and B are two different (real) numbers, then (A+B)/2 is midway between them. This may not be the case in calculator arithmetic. Indeed, the (calculator answer) mean of two numbers may not even be between the two numbers.

To see how this can happen we must look carefully at a calculator's memory. The arithmetic register, the A memory loca-

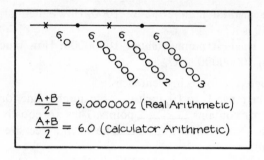

$$\frac{A+B}{2} = 6.0000002 \ (\text{Real Arithmetic})$$

$$\frac{A+B}{2} = 6.0 \ (\text{Calculator Arithmetic})$$

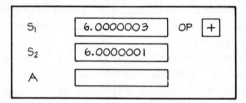

tion, can contain a 16-digit number (in an 8-digit calculator). So the keying sequence

$$6.0000001 + 6.0000003 =$$

actually produces the 9-digit sum 12.0000004 in the A register.

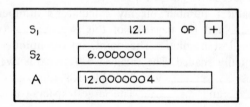

But the calculator must truncate or round this value to 8 digits to store it in S_1 and display it.

$$12.0000004 \xrightarrow[\text{round}]{\text{truncate or}} 12.$$

Thus the calculation:

$$(6.0000001 + 6.0000003) \div 2$$

will produce the answer 6.0 on all 8-digit calculators.

The difference between truncating and rounding has to do with how the least significant digit of a calculation is stored. A calculator which truncates simply throws away extra digits. A calculator that rounds adds one unit to the least significant display digit *if* the oversize part of the number is greater than 5.

For example,

$$\frac{2}{3} = .66666666$$

on a calculator which truncates while

$$\frac{2}{3} = .66666667$$

on a calculator which rounds.

A rounding calculator is slightly more useful because over a large number of chain calculations, the number of round ups and round downs will be about equal; the errors tend to cancel each other out. A truncating calculator always throws the overflow away.

1. Does your calculator round or truncate? Write down a procedure for testing this feature of a calculator. Try it on several different calculators and report the results.

2. Complete the following table. For each row of the table draw a diagram showing the locations of the four numbers on a number line.

A	B	Exact $(A+B)/2$	Calculator $(A+B)/2$	Calculator answer is low	exact	high
25	30	27.5	27.5		x	
10	10.000001	10.0000005				
−10.000001	−10.000000					
95.000000	95.000002					
−95.000002	−95.000000					
95.000003	95.000005					
−95.000005	−95.000003					

3. Suppose that two 8-digit numbers are multiplied together. What is the maximum number of digits needed to record the exact product? Prove your assertion.

4. Notice that $1.000001^2 = 1.00000020000001$. If your calculator has an automatic constant for multiplication observe the display as you key the following.

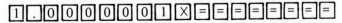

Record each result, and explain why/how this procedure

seems to make the calculator "count" by .0000001's. Devise a similar procedure to make your calculator count by
.0000005's.

5. Real arithmetic satisfies a commutative rule for multiplication. This means that A × B = B × A. Write down five test
problems, and try them on your calculator, to see if you can
find an exception to the commutative rule in calculator arithmetic. Explain your experimental results in light of the fact
that the A register on an 8-digit calculator is 16 digits in
length.

DECIMAL EQUIVALENTS

Every fraction can be expressed as a decimal. Some of the
decimal equivalents terminate, while others do not. The non-
terminating ones eventually repeat, or cycle.

A calculator can be used to compute decimal equivalents
of fractions. For example, on an 8-digit calculator $5 \div 12 =$
.4166666. From this we can guess that $\frac{5}{12} = .416\overline{6}$.

But the calculator quotient $6 \div 17 = .3529411$ does not give
us good insight into the decimal equivalent for $\frac{6}{17}$. What is the
next digit after the two 1's? To get more places in the decimal,

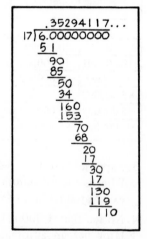

$$\frac{1}{2} = .5$$

$$\frac{1}{3} = .333\cdots \qquad = .\overline{3}$$

$$\frac{2}{3} = .666\cdots \qquad = .\overline{6}$$

$$\frac{1}{4} = .25$$

$$\frac{3}{4} = .75$$

$$\frac{1}{5} = .2$$

long division can be used. Another method is found in problem
4 in the following exercises.

1. Use your memory, a calculator, or paper and pencil to find
decimal equivalents for the following fractions:

a. $\frac{1}{6}$ d. $\frac{7}{8}$ g. $\frac{7}{9}$

b. $\frac{2}{5}$ e. $\frac{1}{9}$ h. $\frac{1}{12}$

c. $\frac{3}{8}$ f. $\frac{3}{11}$ i. $\frac{1}{15}$

2. Study the examples; notice the patterns.

$$\frac{1}{9} = .\overline{1} \qquad \frac{2}{9} = .\overline{2} \qquad \frac{3}{9} = .\overline{3} \qquad \frac{4}{9} = .\overline{4}$$

$$\frac{1}{99} = .\overline{01} \qquad \frac{2}{99} = .\overline{02} \qquad \frac{3}{99} = .\overline{03} \qquad \frac{4}{99} = .\overline{04}$$

$$\frac{1}{999} = .\overline{001} \qquad \frac{2}{999} = .\overline{002} \qquad \frac{3}{999} = .\overline{003} \qquad \frac{4}{999} = .\overline{004}$$

Find fractions with the following decimal equivalents. Use a calculator to check your answers.

a. $.\overline{7}$ c. $.\overline{92}$ e. $.\overline{947}$

b. $.\overline{35}$ d. $.\overline{048}$ f. $.\overline{2917}$

3. Observe that $13.\overline{28} = 13 + .\overline{28}$ or $13 + \frac{28}{99}$ or $\frac{1315}{99}$. Find fractions with the following decimal equivalents. Check using your calculator.

a. $3.\overline{25}$ b. $19.\overline{382}$ c. $8.3\overline{7}$ d. $5.2\overline{43}$

4. The procedure in the flowchart can be programmed for a computer. It produces the digits of the decimal equivalent of a fraction. Use a table to follow the flowchart for N = 6 and D = 17. Find the first ten digits of the decimal for $\frac{6}{17}$.

N	D	Q	R
6	17	3	9
9	17	5	5
5	17	2	9

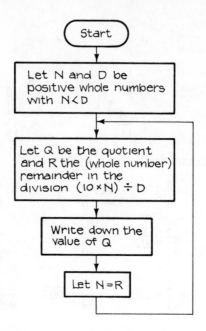

SOLVING EQUATIONS

Many problems can be stated as equations to be solved. Translating an English sentence to a math sentence is an important problem solving skill.

Problem:	Equation (solve for n):
Find a number whose cube is 28.	$n^3 - 28 = 0$
Find a number which when added to the square and cube of itself gives 14.	$n + n^2 + n^3 - 14 = 0$

The guess and check method is widely used in solving equations. The idea is to bracket a solution, and then to narrow in on it. The method requires a lot of calculation, so a calculator or computer is a useful aid. Also, we may not get an exact solution because of calculator arithmetic.

As the bracketing method gets closer and closer to an exact answer, one has to decide when to stop the process. If one

```
          Solve  n² - 19 = 0

  Guess n = 4        4² - 19 = -5
                       Too Low
  Guess n = 5        5² - 19 = 6
                       Too High
  Guess  n = 4.5     4.5² - 19 = 1.25
                       Too High
  Guess  n = 4.3


    and so on
```

decimal place accuracy is desired, stop when the difference between bracket points is .1.

```
             4.3² - 19 = -.51
             4.4² - 19 = +.36

          which is the better
       solution to n² - 19 = 0 ?
```

1. Use the bracketing method to solve the equation $n^2 - 19 = 0$ to *two* decimal place accuracy. (Show your work in detail.)

2. Write equations for the following problems. Then solve to one decimal place accuracy.
   a. Find a number which, when added to the square of itself, gives 13.
   b. Find a number which when subtracted from the square of itself gives 10.

3. Explain why $n^2 + 3 = 0$ does not have a real number solution.

WEIRD EXAMPLES

You should now be convinced that calculator arithmetic is quite a bit different from real arithmetic. Let's look at a few more weird examples. Keep in mind that they are carefully contrived and designed to make small differences evident. In most real world applications, calculator arithmetic and real arithmetic are similar enough to not make an appreciable difference.

The associative rule for addition in real arithmetic is:

$$(A + B) + C = A + (B + C)$$

Use your calculator to try

A = 13.000001

B = 7.0000001

C = 5.0000006

Work the example using an 8-digit calculator. That is, calculate each side of the equation. Your two answers will be different. The difference is small. But it proves that the associative law for addition doesn't always hold on a calculator. The reason is that (A + B) is nine digits in length, so a truncation or rounding error occurs. But the exact value of (B + C) is only eight digits long, so no error occurs there.

1. Try the numbers:

A = 289.13574, B = 83.921827, C = 92.314625

Does the associative rule hold? Is either sum the same as the real arithmetic sum?

2. Try this division example:

99999999/99999998 =

Now find two other positive numbers that are not the same, but whose quotient on a calculator is 1.

Work the following example using an 8-digit calculator. The real arithmetic answer is 7.0000004. Whether the calculator truncates or rounds, the left side and right side answers will be different. The explanation is that (B + C) is nine digits long, so must be truncated or rounded.

The distributive rule for multiplication over addition in real arithmetic:

A × (B + C) = A × B + A × C

Use your calculator to try:
A = .5
B = 6.0000004
C = 8.0000004

1. Use an 8-digit calculator which truncates or rounds each answer to 8 digits. Perform the following addition working from top to bottom and then from bottom to top. Explain why the results differ?

$$
\begin{array}{r}
100.000000 \\
.000003 \\
.000002 \\
.000001 \\
.000002 \\
+ \quad .000002 \\
\hline
\end{array}
$$

2. Consider the calculation
        10000000 × (16.000007 − 9.0000026 − 7.0000044)

Use an 8-digit calculator which does truncated arithmetic, working from left to right inside the parentheses. Compare this calculator result with the exact answer.

3. What is the associative rule for multiplication in real arithmetic? Do you think that it always holds in calculator arithmetic? If not, find an example to support your conclusion.

CALCULATORS VERSUS COMPUTERS

IMPROVING A CALCULATOR

While the simplest four function pocket calculator is a very useful aid to computation, there are many ways to make a calculator even more useful. Adding a square root key, more memory, or making it programmable are examples.

Many companies have total sales in excess of a billion dollars per year. For example, a company's yearly sales may be $3,492,642,800. Since an 8-digit calculator won't handle the larger numbers, many businesses own 12-digit calculators.

1. The U. S. company with the largest yearly sales is American Telephone and Telegraph. Its yearly sales are rapidly approaching a hundred billion dollars. How many digits are needed on a calculator that will deal with such amounts to the nearest dollar?

2. Calculators used in business offices often have a paper tape for displaying answers. As a long column of numbers is added, they are printed on the paper tape to make it easy to check for keying errors.

   An alternative is to construct a calculator with a memory large enough to store all of the numbers in a long sum. After the calculation has been completed, the calculator can display each of the numbers added, one at a time. These can be visibly checked for keying errors.

   Which type of calculator do you think a business person would rather use? Why?

MORE FUNCTION KEYS

A hand held calculator has space for 40 or more keys if they
are small enough. A key can serve two (or even three) purposes,
much like upper and lower keys on a typewriter. Thus a hand
held calculator can be constructed with many dozens of different function keys.

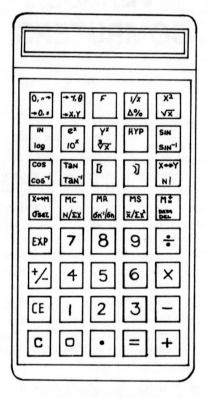

Each function key is designed to solve a specific problem—to
make the problem into a primitive for the calculator user. For
some keys it is easy to learn what problem they solve.

Reciprocal	The $\boxed{1/x}$ key calculates the reciprocal of the number in the S_1 storage location and puts the answer in S_1.
$\boxed{5}$ $\boxed{1/x}$ $\boxed{\rightarrow}$ .2	

Square	The $\boxed{x^2}$ key finds the square of the number in the S_1 memory location and puts the answer in S_1.
$\boxed{8}$ $\boxed{x^2}$ $\boxed{\rightarrow}$ 64	

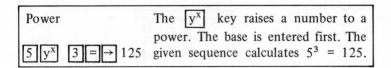

Power   The $\boxed{y^x}$ key raises a number to a
                              power. The base is entered first. The
$\boxed{5}$ $\boxed{y^x}$ $\boxed{3}$ $\boxed{=}$ $\boxed{\rightarrow}$ 125   given sequence calculates $5^3 = 125$.

1. Examine a calculator with a large number of keys. Name and explain several of them, using the style illustrated on this page.

2. What answers would you get after keying in the following problems? (Use a calculator for checking, if it has the keys available.)

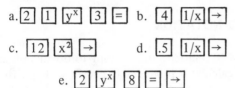

a. $\boxed{2}$ $\boxed{1}$ $\boxed{y^x}$ $\boxed{3}$ $\boxed{=}$ b. $\boxed{4}$ $\boxed{1/x}$ $\boxed{\rightarrow}$

c. $\boxed{12}$ $\boxed{x^2}$ $\boxed{\rightarrow}$ d. $\boxed{.5}$ $\boxed{1/x}$ $\boxed{\rightarrow}$

   e. $\boxed{2}$ $\boxed{y^x}$ $\boxed{8}$ $\boxed{=}$ $\boxed{\rightarrow}$

SCIENTIFIC NOTATION

Scientists often have to deal with very small and very large numbers. Astronomers use the light year as a unit of measure. The speed of light is about 298,000 km per second. A light year is approximately $298,000 \times 60 \times 60 \times 24 \times 365$ km. This calculation will overflow on an 8-digit calculator.

Scientists use scientific notation to deal with numbers of widely varying sizes. The speed of light would be expressed as 2.98×10^5 km/sec. The number .0003287 is expressed as 3.287×10^{-4}. Change these numbers to scientific notation:

   948,730,000   .00314   .0000002564

The star closest to our sun is Alpha Centauri. It is about 4 light years away. Express this in kilometers. At the speed of a fast commercial jet plane (1100 km/hr), how long would it take to fly this distance?

Scientists and engineers generally own calculators that use scientific notation. An 8-digit scientific notation displays many of the numbers in the range −99999999 to 99999999 in the manner to which we have become accustomed. But it can also use the 8-digit display area for scientific notation numbers. This display area can display a signed four digit number with a signed exponent.

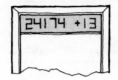

2.4174 +13 means 2.4174×10^{13} (the + may not be displayed)

8.6415 −25 means 8.6415×10^{-25}

Scientific notation calculators often have a 10-digit or 12-digit display area. This allows them to display more significant digits in a scientific notation number.

USING SCIENTIFIC NOTATION

1. What is 893745×97683080? An attempt to do this on an 8-digit or 10-digit calculator produces an overflow. Rewritten in scientific notation the problem becomes (8.93745×10^5) $\times (9.768308 \times 10^7)$. We can mentally calculate $10^5 \times 10^7 = 10^{12}$ and use a calculator to get $8.93745 \times 9.768308 = 87.303764$. The final answer, in scientific notation to 8-digit accuracy, is 8.7303764×10^{13}. Solve the following problems using the same method.

   a. 726164×31648200 c. $.00001234 \times .00005678$

   b. 12345678^2 d. $.0003928 - 847295$

2. The diameter of the earth is about 12,700,000 meters.

   a. The surface area of a sphere is given by $A = \pi d^2$. What is the surface area of the earth?
   b. The population of the earth is about 4.2 billion. There are how many square meters of surface area per person?

3. The average distance from the sun to the earth is 1.5×10^8 km. What is the circumference of a circle with this radius? The earth moves around the sun once in 365.25 days. What is its orbit velocity in km per hour?

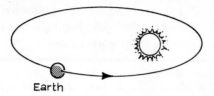

Earth

4. A certain computer can add or subtract two numbers in 1.2×10^{-8} seconds, and it can divide two numbers in 9.4×10^{-8} seconds. How long will it take the computer to do all of the arithmetic in calculating:

$$1 - \frac{1}{2} + \frac{1}{3} - \frac{1}{4} + \frac{1}{5} \cdots - \frac{1}{999998} + \frac{1}{999999} - \frac{1}{1000000}$$

5. A certain virus is shaped much like a rectangular solid, with a length of .00000085 cm, a width of $\frac{1}{10}$ this amount, and a height of $\frac{1}{20}$ the length. Express these dimensions using scientific notation. Find the volume of one such virus. How many would fit in 1 cc?

REPETITION

Have you ever had a job in which you did the same task over and over again? Many jobs are repetitive. A person carrying out the task is a machine-like agent. Indeed, it might be possible to build a machine to do the job.

There are many repetitive computational tasks. Consider a payroll clerk. A worker's hours must be added, and total pay must be calculated. Then withholdings for taxes are calculated and a paycheck is prepared. This must be done for each worker, and it must be done every week. Much of this repetitive task can be done automatically by a computer.

The exercises given below ask you to do some repetitive tasks using a simple calculator. These can also be done on a programmable calculator, one designed to automatically carry out certain repetitive procedures. We discuss programmable calculators in the next section. Computers are especially good at repetitive tasks. A computer can do everything a programmable calculator can do, but also much more.

1. A worker receives the stated hourly rate of pay for the first 40 hours, and 1½ times the rate for additional hours. Time yourself in completing the table. Estimate how long it would take you to process a 1000 worker payroll.

Name	Hours Worked							Total Hours	Pay Rate	Total Pay	With-Holding	Net Pay
	M	T	W	T	F	S	S					
Adams	8.5	8.0	7.5	7.5	8.0			39.5	$4.78	$188.81	12%	$166.15
Jones	7.0	7.5	7.5	7.5	7.0	7.0			$6.49		15%	
Morris		9.0	9.0	9.5	8.5	9.0	4.0		$8.02		18%	
Wilks	6.5	7.5			6.0	7.5	6.5		$5.44		13%	

Total hours for all workers _____

Total pay for all workers _____

Total net pay for all workers   _____

2. A certain bank pays 6% interest compounded quarterly. That is, 1½% interest is added on at the end of each three month period. A person deposits $1000 at the beginning of each quarter for three years, a total of 12 deposits. How much will the person have at the end of three years?

Complete the table, rounding each amount to the nearest cent.

Date	Deposit	Interest	Balance
1 January 1980	$1,000.00	–	$1,000.00
1 April 1980	$1,000.00	$15.00	$2,015.00
1 July 1980	$1,000.00	$30.22	$3,037.22
1 October 1980	$1,000.00	$45.56	
1 January 1981	$1,000.00		
1 April 1981			
1 July 1981			
1 October 1981			
1 January 1982			
1 April 1982			
1 July 1982			
1 October 1982			

3. A man deposits $40,000 in a savings and loan company that pays 8% interest per year, compounded quarterly. At the end of each quarter, just after the interest is paid, the man withdraws $1000. How much will remain in the account at the end of three years, immediately after the 12th withdrawal? Round all money amounts to the nearest cent.

PROGRAMMABLE CALCULATORS

Every calculator contains a number of built-in programs. A program is merely a procedure that a calculator can automatically follow. A calculator follows a built-in program when it multiplies two numbers. Calculators with large numbers of function keys have large numbers of built-in calculator programs.

If a calculation problem occurs frequently for a large number of people, then a calculator company will build a calculator that can automatically solve it. The calculator will have a built-in program that solves the problem, and all the user needs to do is key in the data. Relatively few calculation problems occur frequently enough for this.

An alternative is to make it possible for the calculator user to put new programs into the machine. The user creates a procedure and keys it into the calculator. It is stored in calculator memory and then used much like a built-in function.

There are many programmable calculators on the market. They allow the user to create and key in a program. Some have plug-in memory modules, sold by the calculator company, that contain programs to solve problems in some particular field. For example, one plug-in module may contain programs used in surveying. Another may be useful in navigation, while a third contains entertaining games.

The more expensive programmable calculators have a magnetic card or tape that can be used for permanently storing programs. After a program is keyed into the calculator, the calculator puts a copy of it onto the magnetic storage medium. The program can be input to the calculator at a later time without rekeying. The calculator user can develop a personal library of programs.

USING A PROGRAMMABLE CALCULATOR

Here is an example that illustrates the general ideas involved in using programmable calculators:

A teacher has given three tests. The first test is to count as 18% of the final grade. The second test is to count as 34% of the final grade, while the last test counts as 48% of the final grade. Give a procedure for solving the problem of calculating a student's test weighted score on a calculator:

a. With 4 key memory.

b. That is programmable.

The first step is to understand the problem. Suppose a student has test scores of 67, 75, and 82. The student's weighted score is:

$$.18 \times 67 + .34 \times 75 + .48 \times 82 = 76.92$$

Let's use the notation V1, V2, and V3 for the values of a student's three scores. Then a formula for the weighted score is:

Weighted score $= (.18 \times V1) + (.34 \times V2) + (.48 \times V3)$

Solution using 4-key memory

1. Clear the calculator memory and select a set of scores that have not been processed.
2. Read the first score (V1) and calculate .18 × V1. Add the result to memory.
3. Read the second score (V2) and calculate .34 × V2. Add the result to memory.
4. Read the third score (V3) and calculate .48 × V3. Add the result to memory and then key RM. The weighted score is now in the display. Record it in the grade book.
5. Have all students' been processed? If 'no', go to step 1. Otherwise, stop.

This procedure requires that the numbers .18, .34, and .48 be keyed in for each student. This repetition is avoided on a programmable calculator.

IT'S LESS WORK

Solution using a programmable calculator

If a programmable calculator has been properly programmed for this problem, then proceed as follows:

1. Select a set of scores that have not been processed. Read the value for V1, key it in, and push the **ENTER** key.
2. Read the value for V2, key it in, and push the **ENTER** key.
3. Read the value for V3, key it in, and push the **ENTER** key.

4. The weighted score is now displayed. Record it in the grade book.
5. Have all students' scores been processed? If 'no', go to step 1. Otherwise, stop.

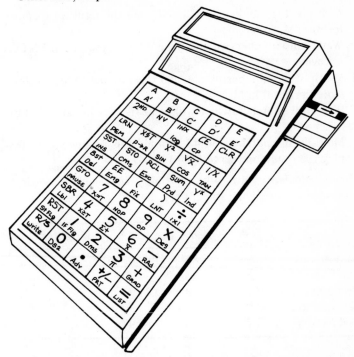

A programmable calculator has memory for storing the program steps. It also has memory for storing numbers occurring in a problem. Thus, the three weights .18, .34, and .48 are stored in calculator memory and used for each student. They do not need to be rekeyed for each student. Therefore, using the programmable calculator is faster than using the 4-key memory system calculator.

This assumes, of course, that the program has been placed into calculator memory. Creating and keying in the program may take quite a bit of time. This time is more than made up in a long repetitive calculation.

CALCULATOR PROGRAM

This is a natural language procedure for the grading program. Details on how to key it into a calculator vary with the calculator. A skilled calculator user could complete the task in about a minute.

1. Wait until a number (which will be V1) is keyed in and **ENTER** is keyed.
2. Multiply the number by .18 and store the result in memory location M.
3. Wait until a number (which will be V2) is keyed in and **ENTER** is keyed.
4. Multiply the number by .34, add this product to M, and then store the result in M.
5. Wait until a number (which will be V3) is keyed in and **ENTER** is keyed.
6. Multiply the number by .48 and add this product to M. Display the result, and go to Step 1.

Use a calculator with 4-key memory to calculate weighted scores for the following student test data.

Name	Test # 1	Test # 2	Test # 3	Weighted Score
Sam Adams	79	84	67	
Sue Davis	98	89	94	
Bob Farley	67	98	92	
Gail Madson	100	85	90	
Ted Nelson	67	98	97	

COMPUTERS

A computer can be thought of as a high speed programmable calculator with some additional enhancements. A major enhancement is adding a typewriter-like keyboard, and a full range of alphabetic characters, for input and output. A computer can work with letters and words as well as with numbers. It is a general purpose automated symbol manipulator.

There is a wide range of electronic digital computing equipment. Included are devices named calculator, programmable calculator, microcomputer, minicomputer, and computer. The price range is approximately $5 to $5 million.

SIMPLE   PROGRAMMABLE   LARGE COMPUTER
CALCULATOR   CALCULATOR   MINICOMPUTER   SYSTEM

$5 $50 $500 $5,000 $50,000 $500,000 $5 MILLION
                       MICROCOMPUTER   MEDIUM SIZED
                                                  COMPUTER SYSTEM

(Note: Each number on this scale is ten times the number to its
left. This is a logarithmic scale.)

At the left end of the scale we have the least expensive
4-function pocket calculators. At the right end of the scale we
have computer systems with a speed of 10 million to 100 million
operations per second. Such a machine can do more calculations
in a minute than a person can do by hand in a lifetime.

At one time there was a clear dividing line between calculators
and computers. All calculators were cheaper than the least
expensive computer. Calculators could only work with numbers,
while computers could work with a full range of alphabetic and
numeric symbols. The price dividing line no longer exists. Some
microcomputers are cheaper than some programmable calculators. Even the "numbers only" versus " works with both letters
and numbers" difference is fading. Some programmable calculators can display letters or words in their output display. Some
microcomputers have a calculator style keyboard and are easily
portable, like a calculator.

A computer solves a problem by following a step by step set
of directions, called a computer program. A computer can
automatically follow a program that has been stored in its primary memory. Primary memory on a computer is like the
memory that is built into a calculator or programmable calculator. It can be used to store a program, data to be processed
(numbers and letters or words) and answers produced by a
calculation.

Most computer systems also have a secondary memory. It
can store a larger quantity of data and programs than can primary memory. Magnetic tape, much like a hi-fi system uses, is
one form of secondary storage. The magnetic coating used on
magnetic tape can be used to coat a flat circular aluminum
plate. This plate spins rapidly and is called a magnetic disk. Magnetic disks are a widely used form of secondary storage for
computer systems.

COMPUTER EXERCISES

1. Computer scientists use the letter K to stand for the number
   2^{10}. What is the value of K? A very small computer system
   may have primary memory that will store 8K or 16K characters (letters, digits, or punctuation marks). What is the value
   of 8K? Consider a single spaced typewritten page, 72 charac-

ters per line, and 50 lines per page. Express the number of characters in terms of K.

2. A large computer system, costing $1 million to $5 million, may have primary memory that can store 1024 K or more characters. What is the value of 1024 K? Select a long novel and estimate its length in characters. Express this in terms of K and compare it with the primary memory capacity of a large computer system.

3. The storage capacity of computer magnetic tape is often expressed as a number of characters per inch. Microcomputers sometimes use inexpensive cassette tape recorders which have a tape speed of $1\frac{7}{8}$ inches per second. Suppose a tape has a playing time of 15 minutes, and is recorded at a density of 32 characters per inch. Find the capacity of the tape.

4. Large computer systems often use more expensive magnetic tape systems. The tape is ½ inch wide and a full reel is 2400 feet in length. Recording densities of 800 characters per inch, 1600 characters per inch, or 6250 characters per inch are used. Find the capacity of a tape recorded at each of these densities. A 500 page novel contains about 1 million characters. How many 500 page novels could be stored on one tape at each recording density?

5. A magnetic disk pack consists of several flat circular plates, coated with recording material. The plates are stacked one above the other, with air space between to allow access by read/write leads. A disk pack that will store 300 million characters costs about $400. A 2400 foot reel of tape that can be recorded at a density of 6250 characters per inch costs about $15. Calculate the cost per character of storage of each of these secondary storage media.

6. An inexpensive microcomputer system, costing perhaps $600, can perform about 10,000 multiplications in one second. A very large computer system, costing perhaps $5 million, can perform about 10 million multiplications in one second. Compare the two machines in terms of their cost relative to their speeds. Suggest some reasons one might buy the more expensive machine.

COMPUTER SCIENCE

The first general purpose electronic digital computer was completed in December, 1945. Now there are hundreds of thousands of them. Millions of people use computers in their everyday lives.

It is easy to learn to use computers programs written by other people. Most computing centers maintain a large library of those programs. A person who has never used a computer can learn to use a library program in a few minutes. It is only slightly more difficult than learning to use a function key such as y^x on a calculator.

In the 1960's many colleges and universities established computer science departments. Quite a few high schools began to give computer courses. These were designed for people who want to learn how to write computer programs and to know more about uses of computers.

There are two aspects to learning to program a computer. One has to learn a language that the machine can understand (act as an agent for). And one has to learn to write programs (that is, procedures) to solve problems. There are many different programming languages. *BASIC* is easy for students to learn and is most widely used at the precollege level. *COBOL* is the most widely used language for programming solutions to business problems. Languages such as *FORTRAN* and *PASCAL* tend to be preferred by scientists. Once one has learned one programming language, it is much easier to learn a second or third.

Learning to solve problems (to design procedures) is a major part of computer science. Most of what one learns about problem solving is not dependent upon any particular programming language or computer. Problem solving techniques and knowledge of the problem field are necessary. All of one's education contributes to improving problem solving skills.

Computer science is more than just writing programs to solve problems. A college student majoring in computer science may take coursework in many of the following areas:

1. **Computer Graphics.** A computer can use a television-like screen or a pen and ink plotter to draw graphs, charts, engineering or architectural drawings.

2. **Information Retrieval.** A collection of data or information is called a data bank. It may consist of journals and books, statistical data, or airline reservation information. Computers are widely used to store and access such data banks.

3. **Digital Electronics.** Most colleges of engineering offer coursework on computer circuitry. It leads to an understanding of the details of how the circuitry works and how to design better computers.

4. **Artificial Intelligence.** Computers can play chess and checkers, respond to questions in English, do medical diagnostic work, etc. All of these are aspects of artificial intelligence.

5. **Simulation.** A major aspect of all sciences is developing formulas and models that describe or predict happenings in the field. The use of computers in this descriptive/predictive mode is called computer simulation.

6. **Numerical Analysis.** Many math problems can be solved by use of a computer. This field of study is called numerical analysis. It combines the study of math and computers.

Computer science is a large and rapidly growing field. Computers are useful in almost every aspect of business, government, industry, and education. The number of computers is growing very rapidly, and new uses are continually being discovered. Because of this it is likely that computers will have a major impact upon your life.

COMPUTER ACTIVITIES

1. Microcomputers are now quite common in people's homes and in schools. Find someone who has a microcomputer in his/her home. How is it used?

2. Interview two or three acquaintances to see if their occupation involves use of a computer. Find out what they know about computers, and how they learned it.

3. It is possible to build computer circuitry, primary memory, and secondary memory into a typewriter. This is now being done, to help secretaries do their typing work. Make a list of tasks or problems that a computerized typewriter might help solve. A computerized typewriter system is called a word processing system.

4. Examine the Yellow Pages of a telephone book. Select 10 companies/businesses at random. For each, write a brief statement of the type of work they do. Then write a brief discussion as to the possible usefulness of a computer in that business. Check the entries under computers. If there is a computer store in your area, visit it and find out about the machines that they sell.

5. The term *computer literacy* refers to a knowledge of the capabilities, limitations, and applications of computers. There are now many excellent books designed to help people become more computer literate. If you have enjoyed this *Problem Solving With Calculators* text, then you will enjoy *Are You Computer Literate?* by Billings and Moursund. It is published by dilithium Press.

INTERFACE AGE™ MAGAZINE

For Businessmen...
Professionals...
Students...
You...

Happiness is...a computer magazine you can understand

Step into the exciting world of computing with INTERFACE AGE Magazine. Written and edited expressly for those who want to get more out of their life and business through the use of computers. Join the 85,000 plus who make reading INTERFACE AGE a priority each month. Enjoy articles that not only tell you how, but show you how. Each issue of INTERFACE AGE contains projects, programs, games and reports on and about people and their computers.

Learn how easy it is to own and operate your own computer system at home or in your business. Explore the many ways a computer can make money for you. Keep up to date with the latest new products and developments. Only INTERFACE AGE brings you all this plus much, much more.

The magazine leading the way. . .
bringing people and technology together

#2284-48
1981
5-50
C